NOT

Another

Singles

Book

A Guide to Living Single in a Dating World:
Love yourself and BECOME the person you are looking
for

NOT Another Singles Book

Book 1 of NOT Another Singles Series

www.lavoniartryon.com

Copyright Page

Copyright © 2020 by [**LaVonia R. Tryon**]

NOT Another Singles Book
Book 1 of NOT Another Singles Series

trained professional before making any decision regarding treatment of yourself or others.

NOT

Another

Singles

Book

Second Edition

La Vonia R. Tryon

Contents

FOREWORD

"Not Another Singles Book" validates its name by breaking the chain of writings suggesting that being single is some condition that needs to be escaped from and looks at it through the lens of someone who understands its impact on the lives of those who are wrestling with its truths.

Being single is an important time to prepare us for marriage. It can also be a time to experience a closer communion with GOD. As we seek GOD to cleanse us of the world and help us become the kind of wife or husband that would bless someone, we will soon find we have learned how to be content with Him. One thing for sure—it is better to be alone with Jesus than to spend your life with somebody who doesn't love you or Jesus. Marriage has to be based on decisions directed by the Holy Spirit, but when it is based on our emotion or our perceived need; we often come up sorry. The greatest mistake you will ever make is to rush for marriage and lose your peace. The greatest admonish I have ever heard about choosing a partner in marriage is found in 2 Corinthians 6:14 when it says, "Be ye not unequally yoked together with unbelievers: for what fellowship hath righteousness with unrighteousness? And what communion hath light with darkness?" Whom you connect with will determine whom you serve. You can't disobey GOD in your choice of a mate and expect Him to bless your marriage. You can do bad all by yourself.

Not Another Singles Book is a simplistic yet riveting look at "Singleness" as a way that few have been able to deliver. It is a must read for every person who is confronted by any form of singleness, whether through lifestyle, counseling, or even if you are called to mentor single persons of any age.

LaVonia Tryon's life is a proven testament of the power of God operating through someone determined to serve and please Him. There are some single people who are miserable because their desire to get "a mate from God" is greater than their desire for God, and it dominates their lives. They have prayed and prayed, yet they still have no mate. As a result, some of them settle for Satan's provision instead of asking GOD for the patience to wait for the one whom HE would send. If they would look to JESUS and seek to please HIM, rather than being concerned about a mate, soon they would find the right one crossing their path, or they will find that God will provide something better in their lives.

LaVonia has made it evident that you can enjoy life in God without your world being dominated by the pressure of finding the "life boat" of marriage. The transparency she delivers in these pages will surely prove to be life changing to those who understand her present frustrations and are facing similar struggles and triumphs of being single.

Charles E. Rodgers
Charles E. Rodgers, BA, MA, ME, D. Min.
Senior Pastor, Hope Community Church
Professor of Church History, Birmingham Theological
Seminary

How to Read This Book

C'mon LaVonia. Will you just get to the book already?

Just a few strong suggestions to get the most out of our time together. I really want my heart for this book and the vision that God gave to come across as authentic as possible and I believe 2 key steps will assist you in getting into your Singleness before you get out of it. And if you aren't Single, yet you find yourself reading this book, I believe that these suggestions will help you too.

Accountability.
Nobody wants to be Single alone. Read it again and let it sink in. Being Single is a status, being alone is a choice, and not a good one, might I add (Genesis 2:18 wasn't about marriage, it was about relationship). Get you a girlfriend or a homeboy or two to read this book with. You can turn it into a book club, Bible study or book of the month amongst friends. If you need a little bit of help convincing them to read the book – send them the link on my website at www.lavoniartryon.com to get a free download of the first 3 chapters of this book and the download of the Workbook (coming November 2020). Trust me, they'll join.

Application.
It's proven by studies everywhere (just pick one) that you retain more when you take notes. Now, I'm not saying God is gonna ask for your sermon notes when you get to Heaven, but I'm not saying He's *not* not gonna ask for them, either. Seriously, take the time to do the work. Go to www.lavoniartryon.com to download your Workbook (coming November 2020).

Confessions of a Reformed Serial Monogamist

What qualifies me to write this book? Nothing in and of myself has made me an expert on Singleness, unless you count the fact that I have *always* been in a relationship—although never made it down the aisle.

When God called me to write this book, I tried to rationalize my way out of it. It started as a note on a social media site and then became a blog of my thoughts. Finally, when I sat down and wrote 20 pages in one day, I realized that I couldn't escape it. Writing this book has been a labor of love because I truly believe that God has given me a passion and a heart for Singles. I know the wisdom that He has imparted in me, much of it gained by going about things the wrong way, will help someone else that's on this journey of what is commonly called the "in between" phase. Many things that I have gone through, the Master Teacher had to teach me again and again, but hopefully my struggles will turn into your lessons.

However, I would be less than honest if I didn't disclose that this book has also been a burden for me. It has brought me to tears, causing me to literally wrestle with God, because I didn't want to share everything He was requiring of me. I have been called to be shamelessly transparent in these pages and (although sometimes kicking and screaming), I have submitted to the Lord's will.

The scariest part about opening up about my struggles, fears, experiences and even my triumphs in this book, was not for fear that people who don't know me would read it. I was more concerned about the people that do know me; those that I see on a daily basis, that I sit across the table from, that I minister to and labor with. I felt like exposing the shortcomings that led to the revelations I have discovered would disqualify me in their eyes—that somehow I would now look different.

God confirmed that I would look different to them; I would become more relatable. I believe that a person's ministry is only as effective as their ability to relate to the audience to whom they are ministering. For some reason, because I am now content in my Singleness, although I'm still in this journey, some people have assumed that I was "there"; that I was all put together. This is the furthest thing from the truth. All the struggles and the heartache and the break ups (and make ups and break ups again), lead me to what you see now. We should never forget that we are all being transformed from glory to glory. We have to learn to give God glory in our Single state so that He can give us peace in it. Don't forget where you see a person now is not where they have always been.

I believe that by sharing in my struggles, you can also share in my joys. Many things I went through and things you'll soon read about were hard lessons I had to learn, but they are things that you may be spared from going through. Learn from my experiences. If through my transparency, you can be encouraged, then sharing my story with those who have found themselves in or may still be in the same cycle I have been delivered from will be worth it.

So, why the title NOT Another Singles Book? Simply because it is not. I guarantee you that this book will be different from any other book you have ever read on Singleness. Why? First, it is written for Singles by an actual Single. I've read many a book about Singleness written by people who aren't actually Single. Theoretically, this isn't wrong, but in reality, it gets kind of annoying. I know I am not the only person that has been irritated by a married person telling me how to manage my Single life. Mind you, that person was Single before at some point, so their advice can actually be very useful. However, when you are here and they are there, sometimes it can feel like someone already in the lifeboat, telling you to keep swimming. Great advice, but what we really want is help into the boat.

That is what this book will prayerfully give you—help into the boat. Not necessarily into the "marriage" boat, but into the "satisfied" boat (or at the very least, throw you a life jacket to make the journey a little easier).

Though Singleness may not be your permanent address, it's your current address. Unless you have gotten a revelation from the Lord, you don't know how long you will be here; so you might as well unpack your bags. Prayerfully by the end of this book, you will think of your Singleness as a gift and stop trying to get out of it—before you actually get into it.

So to answer the initial question, by the world's standards, maybe I'm not qualified, but I serve a God that is and He chooses to use whomever He pleases. I am humbled that He trusted me enough. He brought me out of the pit of loneliness, rejection and identity crisis, so that I could then turn and encourage someone else[1]. This is my reasonable service.

This 2nd edition is one that I am blessed to produce. I wanted to stay true to the original manuscript, so you will only see minor revisions. In the last 3 years since the original publication, God has done so much in my life, but you will have to read my second book to find out! I love each and every one of you reading this. Thank you for making my reality better than my dreams.

Journeying Together,
La Vonia

---

[1] Luke 22:31-32

~1

I'm Single—Not a Leper

Sometimes I wish everyone were single like me-a simpler life in many ways!...God gives the gift of the single life to some, the gift of the married life to others.
~1 Corinthians 7:7 MSG

Sometimes you have to stand alone to prove that you can still stand. ~Anonymous

Throw away everything negative that you have ever thought or heard about Singleness. If you were ever told that being Single was a lesser calling, you were horribly misinformed! Singleness is a blessing, not a curse. I know that this may be so far from what you have been taught and trained, even in church… *especially* in church.

We as Singles are taught that Singleness is an "in-between" phase—a mere holding ground until we get married. This is in direct conflict with what God has said in 1 Corinthians 7:35. God says that our period of Singleness is a time of undistracted devotion to Him. This is a time that God has set apart to create and develop you into a whole person—to mold you into the person that He began to shape in your mother's womb. He has a plan for your Singleness and it has nothing to do with getting you out of it! You haven't gotten into it yet!

Using Singleness as a holding ground is like getting a job with a contract and not decorating your office, not making business cards, not even setting up your voicemail because you know that this is not your permanent position. Who does that?! No one! If you know that you will be in a place for a while, you get comfortable and make it your own. Even people who stay in hotels use the drawers and closets. What am I saying? Settle in. Get comfortable. Decorate your Single life.

~Our Viewpoint Compared to God's~

Why do we have a negative view of Singleness in the first place? Has this always been the case? I don't think so. Somewhere down the line, we were taught to believe that marriage is the better, if not the best calling and that every Single person longs to get married as soon as possible. If not, then something is deathly wrong with us. But again, why is this? This mindset had to originate somewhere.

I believe if we really quiet ourselves and search deep within we will find where that notion originated. This viewpoint either arose from a warped view of marriage as expressed on a television screen, an observation or study of other couples, the imagined deafening tick of our biological clock, or maybe the overwhelming stirrings of sexual appetites often caused by sexual immorality—Somewhere! God did not place this negative view in your head and I challenge you to find a scripture anywhere that confirms it. Go on… I'll wait...You back yet? Exactly! There is not a single scripture where God admonishes Singleness or even one where it is anything less than honored.

Now, for the analytical ones, I can hear you say, "Well, it is the first thing that God called 'not good' during creation." Be careful how you interpret that scripture[1]. God did not say that Adam's singleness was not good, but rather He states that Adam being alone was not good. Big difference! Of course, God then (after giving Adam a job and purpose) created his helpmeet, called "woman", which was Eve, so that they could fulfill the command given to all God's living creation: to be fruitful and multiply[2]. I don't believe that God was implying that Adam shouldn't have been Single in the time frame that he was. His Singleness was definitely a calling and we will explore that more in Chapter 8.

Therefore, if the Bible is the living, inerrant, infallible Word of God[3] and His Word says that our Singleness is a gift in the sense that we have the freedom of being completely Kingdom minded[4], then our negative view has to be in direct conflict with what God wants for us. It is indeed a gift, which as the Giver intended, has a distinct purpose.

I believe the gift of Singleness can be broken down into three categories: gifts that are for a reason and considered short term, gifts for a season and may have extended use, and gifts for a lifetime that are meant to be savored. As with natural gifts, some gifts such as food or a time-sensitive gift certificate are meant for immediate use. If you wait too long to use the gift, you run the risk of it expiring or spoiling before you have had the opportunity to enjoy it.

---

[2] Genesis 2:18-24

[3] Timothy 3:16

[4] 1 Corinthians 7:34

If used as it is purposed and within it's time frame, it satisfies and is enjoyed. If not, you are left wishing you would have used it or consumed it while you had the chance. Singleness can be likened to this scenario. Your Single season, if God has marriage in His plan for you, has an expiration date, which is the day you stand at the altar. You want to be able to say you used all of your Singleness for its purpose, before it "expired" and you were left with a bad taste in your mouth, pun intended.

There are also those gifts that are meant to be enjoyed over time. For example, perfume and clothing, depending on how well or how often you use it will determine the length of time you have it. In the case of perfume, the more you use it, the more you are associated with that particular scent. Some things get better with time. Your Singleness may be a gift that has grown better in time, either because you are just deciding to get into it, or because you have allowed God to change your mindset and have begun to use it for its intended purpose.

Decide to let your Singleness be the sweet aroma that is associated with you, not the stench of a lifestyle that you don't enjoy. Women can attest that the same fragrance can smell a certain way on one individual, but completely different on another. Our Singleness has a distinct aroma. The question is whether it is attracting people to ourselves and a life devoted to Christ, or if its odor is deterring others from seeking their own unique scent in Singleness.

Lastly, there are those gifts that are for a lifetime. Because it is rare to receive a gift that will span a lifetime, this gift should be cherished. It's your grandmother's pearls or your great great-uncle's pocket watch: kept in a special place and often displayed, but only to be handled with extreme care for fear its value will depreciate. For those blessed with the gift of Singleness, those whose lives are totally devoted to service in God with no desire for marriage for the sake of the Kingdom, this gift is truly priceless. Your Single life is one that should be displayed and used as an example of a life "souled" out for Christ. Again, I must say that this gift is rare and not to be looked upon as a curse, but as a powerful manifestation of the plan that God has specially for you, and the trust He has bestowed upon you, knowing your ability to handle it well. Please recognize the favor God has granted you.

So, if we can now agree that Singleness is indeed a gift (fitting into one of the aforementioned categories), then when we choose not to use it as such, we are spiritually rewrapping it in its original packaging, putting "Return to Sender" on it and shipping it back to the Giver[5]. Not only is this tacky and ungrateful, but it may make the Giver question if He should devote more time and effort to give us another gift after we were so callous with the first. Remember, He that is trusted with little is then trusted with much.[6]

Now that we see from God's viewpoint Singleness is not a curse, let's discuss how we came to view it as such. I believe that in the same way misery loves company-happiness seeks companions. Let's discuss this in a bit more detail.

First, there are those individuals who are happy in their relationships and want us to experience the same joy they have. There is nothing malicious about their intentions; they just want us Singles to join them in their coupledom, so that we can all double date and talk about relationships

---

[5] Matthew 25:24-25

[6] Luke 16:10-12

and how great our "boos" are. It's hard to understand how we can be truly comfortable Single and not want what they have. Although their goal is to share their joy, the result is usually just the opposite and increases our awareness that we are indeed a "table of 1."

Next are those people who are Single, but aren't content and can't understand how you can be satisfied in your status because they are so unhappy in theirs. Quite naturally, if they can't get out of their Singleness the least they can do is help you out of yours, so they can live vicariously through you. They try to accomplish this in several ways, whether it's by setting you up with friends, family members or the 'cast-offs' that they weren't interested in. Their goal is to get you hooked up and off the Single market because, "it's so hard to find a good man/woman nowadays." It is a foreign concept that you are content where you are—how could you be? You're alone and lonely just like them and they are anything but happy.

I challenge you to seek to change their mindset. Encourage them (and yourself) to understand there is a difference between being alone and being lonely. Alone signifies that you are in your own company and there is no one with you at a particular point in your life. Loneliness states that you are miserable and empty because of it. Although they have the same root word, they carry two very different meanings especially for a Single. Being alone does not mean you have to be lonely. We will discuss this concept more in a later chapter.

~Content Doesn't Equate to Crazy~

Now let's talk about the married folks. Although they mean well, they often only succeed in making us overtly aware of our Singleness. A married man told me recently that something must be wrong with me if I'm 29 and still Single. "Are you crazy?!" he asked incredulously. Before I gave an equally offensive response, I paused and thought about it… "*AM I Crazy*?! Am I? I mean, I have met some amazing men in my lifetime. Some I've dated and others, ummm…not so much, yet I'm still Single. What happened with Peter? and Billy? and Mike?"

Before long, I was replaying old relationships in my head and trying to figure out what went wrong. What did *I* do to mess it up? Some of those answers were easier to find than others. But then (mind you, all of this is racing through my head while he is still droning on about his grandmother's theory on women that are approaching their 30's but still unmarried), I thought about something my Bishop told me, the very one who wrote the forward. "Many people want a wedding, but they have no idea that they are getting a marriage."

A wedding is when everyone smiles at you and tells you that this is the happiest day of your life. A marriage is when you have to pull out that old album to remind yourself that you have had happier days. A wedding is a big white dress and freshly pressed suit with everyone waiting on you, taking care of your every whim. A marriage is both of you working 40+ hours, picking up the baby from daycare, preparing dinner, washing a load of laundry while you bathe the children, ironing clothes for the morning, all while preparing for your 9 AM meeting. The wedding is the sales pitch, but the marriage is the reality and we know nothing is ever quite the same as it's advertised. After finally coming back to my senses, I looked at the man and said, "Nope I'm not, but obviously you are." I'm not saying marriage is crazy, but I am saying that it takes a lot more work than I believe our Single minds can even fully comprehend. Only a perfect God can take two totally separate lives, combine them with His vision, then give us back one whole life. Now, that's crazy.

~A Labeled Leper~

If that's not your story, maybe you have encountered the married person who feels it's their God-ordained duty to get you out of the pit of Singleness by hooking you up with every single guy at their church, or their bridge partners' son, or any available doctor, or the deacon's grandson that "comes to church more often than not".

The church often times makes us feel worse about our status instead of helping us understand our purpose in it. Even Ruth had a church mother who was more concerned with her marital status than her calling in God[7]. Naomi seemed more focused on Ruth being able to re-marry than she was on the cultivation of Ruth's newfound relationship with God. Many times those who are more "seasoned" in the Lord, or even just in their personal marital status, forget that as Singles our devotion is to God first and not to our desire to find a mate. We will come back to Ruth's story at the end of this book.

We often feel like lepers, outcasts, and ostracized by the church as the "in between" group. As a result, the Singles ministry has begun to be looked at as being all about hook-ups, and people join because they are looking for their husbands (yep I said that right). Being the Singles Ministry leader at my past church for 2 years, I can attest to this on some level. In fact, several men informed me that the reason they didn't join the Singles Ministry is because they

---

[7] Ruth 1:9-12

felt outnumbered (meetings and events are often 10-1 in favor of women) and that many women were "after" them.

I first laughed at this notion like it couldn't be true and they had to be paranoid. Now I'm finding that, although it may be exaggerated, their viewpoint definitely had validity. Many women have grown tired of the wait and are now, either directly or indirectly, the aggressor. For men, this goes against their natural instincts to be the leader and pursuer, so what other choice do they have but to tuck tail and run? A note should be added that this may not apply to all men, but usually to the ones that we want to be found by.

Although the Singles Ministry at my church is focused on leading other Singles into a deeper relationship with God through discipleship, evangelism and fellowship, there is an underlying current that we (and I said we) do desire marriage. It manifests in our discussion groups and in the books that we choose for discipleship—even in our everyday conversations. Some of us hide it better than others, but it's still there, just below the surface. I believe my personal calling as the Singles leader was to facilitate the balance between desiring marriage and actively serving God during this season.

We shouldn't have to wear a sign that says we're Single, but sometimes we feel like we are wearing a bull's-eye vest with a target on our foreheads. We will often hear, "Your husband/wife is just around the corner "or "Just hold on baby," or "If I had known when I was Single what I know now, I would have waited." That last statement is what I want to take and focus a majority of the remaining chapters on: "If I would have known." If you would have known what?! That is what is screaming in practically every Single person's head when we hear that. No one ever tells us how to get to contentment, just that we need to get there. Well, keep reading. Maybe I can help.

I pray that while you are reading this book and if in this chapter alone you've seen the very place that you are and you desperately want to get out of it, that you will come to understand contentment in your Singleness by the end. If these struggles resonate within your spirit, I pray you get a better idea of what contentment looks like as you continue in your journey. For those of you that have allowed others that aren't content in their Singleness to shake yours, I challenge you to inspire them to find contentment in their own Singleness. Make it evident that you are using it as a time to draw closer to God; bring them over to your side instead of slumming on theirs. And if you happen to be one of the miserable Single ones, then prayerfully this book will awaken in you a desire to find your place in this season, whether permanently or temporarily.

~2

I'm Complete… Alone

…and you are complete in Him, who is the head of all principality and power.
~Colossians 2:10, NKJV

I don't like to be labeled lonely just because I'm alone.
~Delta Burke

I am complete alone. Four words easier said than believed, especially amongst Christian Singles. If I am complete, why do I feel so broken? Why am I so alone? Where does the loneliness come from? The majority of Christians will face these questions along this Single journey. Although they may seem unanswered, I've discovered we are often only looking in the wrong place. If you don't feel complete, maybe it's because you have forgotten the most important component of this concept: your completion has to come from Christ. You will always feel lonely and broken and alone (even if you do get married), until you realize that only God can fill you. Relationship by definition symbolizes a connection, not completion. The only person that can complete you is the One who first created you, and then took on human form to die for you, just to redeem you back to Himself. That's completion.

~The Permeable Membrane~

This is not something that I learned overnight, and is something that I have to remind myself continuously. Contentment is not a destination, but a journey towards understanding the purpose of our Singleness and becoming complete in Christ, even while we expectantly desire to be someone's complement. Easier said than done, and I have the failed relationships to prove it. I struggled for a long time trying to find my identity, and often defining it in the man I was dating.

Elizabeth Gilbert has a concept in her book (also a Motion Picture) *Eat Pray Love* of the Permeable Membrane:

"To have issues with boundaries, one must have boundaries in the first place, right? But I disappear into the person I love. I am the permeable membrane. If I love you, you can have everything. You can have my time, my devotion, my money, my family, my dog, my dog's money, my dog's time—everything. If I love you, I will carry for you all your pain, I will assume your own insecurity, I will project upon you all sorts of good qualities that you have never actually cultivated in yourself and I will buy Christmas presents for your entire family… I will give you all of this and more, until I get so exhausted and depleted that the only way I can recover my energy is by becoming infatuated with someone else."

I related so much with this statement that I started crying watching this scene in the movie. She had just described the way I had approached every relationship in my life,

23

until about three years ago. I didn't know who I was; I was merely a reflection of the person I was dating which was why I was never Single—*Ever*. I took on a different personality in every relationship, some easier to adapt to than others. I did everything, said everything, and became everything that he was looking for. I molded myself into his perfect mate, whomever he happened to be at that time. Now, some of you may be wondering (and if you are, please refer back to the tagline on the cover), "Well, what's wrong with that?!" OK, let's start with the obvious answer: I'm STILL Single! So something didn't work out with my game plan.

Secondly, and most importantly, Christ never intended for us to find our identity in anyone but Him. He states that we are made in His image[8], created as His workmanship[9] and that our very being is in Him[10]. There is no way we can be that to, or for someone else. God intends for us to have our identity and character deeply rooted in Him before we are joined with someone else.

You first have to be complete in Christ! This cannot be stressed enough. One of the problems that I had with trying to be everything to the man that I was dating was that it was physically and emotionally exhausting. Albeit, I will confess that it was a bit easier for me because I didn't know who I was to begin with, so it wasn't that far of a stretch to play a particular character role for him. I had no baseline. I was who he needed or wanted me to be without even realizing it.

---

[8] Genesis 1:26

[9] Ephesians 2:10

[10] Acts 17:28

We discussed in the previous chapter the concept of the proverbial hook-ups. There is nothing directly wrong with this, but it can get dangerous if we become so focused on being hooked up that we begin asking friends, family, church members, co-workers, friends' boyfriends—*Everyone*—if they "know someone that would be good for me?" Our mindset becomes clouded with fantasies of being in a relationship and we confirm what everyone else is saying. We start to believe all the hype. In the famous words of Frank Sinatra, "We are nobody unless and until someone loves us, so we better find ourselves someone to love."[11] I was right there and almost married the wrong guy because of this false belief. It's natural to want a relationship and desire companionship. We were created that way, but it can't be a consuming thought.

This is one of the major mistakes that I made in my engagement. Gasp! Yep, I was engaged. Bet you can figure out how that ended. I assumed the role that he was used to; the one he needed the most. In this case, that role happened to be caretaker. He never really had to be head of a household or make decisions and provide for himself, before he met me. It was a role that if I had encouraged him to develop, or allowed him to truly pursue me (discussed in Chapter 8), he would have probably learned.

But, why bother? I could just take on that role, then he wouldn't have to change and we could skip all of the messy growing pains. Right? Wrong! What I didn't realize is that once I assumed the role, I would have to maintain it for the entire span of the relationship. While I was so busy convincing him that I was "the one," I didn't have the time or energy to realize that he wasn't completely sure of himself as a man. He had yet to find his place in this world,

---

[11] Frank Sinatra- When Somebody Loves You

so he had no problem with taking up residence in the fantasy of mine.

He was so caught up in the web that I had spun for him that when I would try to return to reality (where the real me would fight for breath), it would shake his whole world because it contradicted the "me" he had fallen in love with. He now not only approved of me as "his one," he had begun to invest his hopes, dreams, and happiness into me. Can you imagine the pressure of having to keep up the charade of being perfect or at least perfect for him? If his happiness depended on me, when I had a bad day his world was shattered. When I wasn't up to being his strength and needed him to be strong for me, he was incapable of doing that because to be my support system went against the very nature of the foundation *I* had built.

The whole relationship was built on my strength, my happiness, and my fantasy world, which falsely advertised that I could be all these things for him. It was destined to fail because anything not built on the solid Rock will wash away in the slightest storm[12]. Needless to say, I couldn't handle the pressure of being responsible for all of someone's happiness. No one but Christ can support that type of weight. So, it didn't end well.

Ugly story, huh? Imagine living it. I'm sharing this with you because I don't wish for anyone else to go through the same thing. My struggle—your lesson. This is one of those, "If I would have known then what I know now" moments.

It was a hard life lesson to learn, but surprisingly the only thing that I would change about it was how much I hurt him. I wouldn't change the pain I experienced, because God opened my eyes to the fact that marriage had become

---

[12] Matthew 7:24-27

an idol for me. I don't know if I would have seen how deeply it was rooted in me from just reading a book or attending a seminar. Some things I believe are better taught with experience.

How could I idolize marriage? Simply stated, anything that we desire more than God and His will for us has become a graven image. We will discuss how marriage can become an idol and how we can bring it back into perspective in Chapter 3.

~Iron Sharpens Iron but Cuts Paper~

With hindsight being 20/20, I realized how the two other major relationships that I had been in up to this point were different. Both previous beaus were solid in their identities, established in both Christ and the world, so neither one of them resided in my created fantasy—they only vacationed there. This is a major difference because unlike my ex-fiancé, they recognized that although the vacation relationship was nice and breezy and trouble free, it could only sustain for a short amount of time before the responsibilities of the real world started weighing in.

They realized the representative of me was simply that, a carbon copy, a mere advertisement of the person I could be for them without any of the commitment of permanency. I was Cancun; an all-expense paid fantasy getaway of a relationship, lacking the responsibilities, pitfalls, and even the triumphs of something real. This was why I was always more invested then they were, which made it so much harder for me to let go when it was over.

The beautiful tragedy of a vacation is that all the investment is in the advertising, in the pitch. The hope is that if all the best attractions and benefits are shown at the beginning, you will have no choice but to participate. There is no mystery. Every possible experience that you can have is laid out on display for you to pick. This is how I began every relationship. I pulled out all stops in a very short time, hoping to hook him and make him realize what a great catch I was. The part that I didn't and couldn't understand was that, just like a vacation, once all the exhibits have been visited, restaurants experienced, and landmarks explored, it loses its appeal and the person leaves, heading back to reality. Vacations were never meant to be permanent.

We must realize that no human relationship can be perfect at all times, unless one or both parties have conceded that in order to keep the illusion of peace, they will forfeit their individuality. I only recently became aware that I was the one doing this. It now strikes me as ironic that my constant string of "boos" figured it out and got out before I even realized I was doing it. I believe this was the root of many of my breakups and not the actual superficial reason that we told each other as we parted ways.

No one can stay on vacation forever no matter how blue the skies are. Ask yourself how many times you have met a person and questioned, "She/He's too perfect; something has to be wrong," or "This is too good to be true." And what happened? You found a flaw or uncovered something that you didn't love, but you learned to deal with—if it was worth it. I believe that in every relationship friction is evident even if it isn't negative. Iron sharpens iron[13]. We must understand that in order to get sharp, our irons must grind against each other, removing the dull areas to make

---

[13] Proverbs 27:17

smooth. This is not often a fluffy, happy, butterflies-in-the-wind, easy-does-it process. It's work, as is every real relationship we will ever participate in, romantic or platonic. This is not to say that the relationship should be plagued with drop down, drag out, full-fledged fights. That's not healthy either. There has to be a balance. When two complete persons decide to share lives, know that in order to remain fresh, your iron will have to be sharpened.

~You Must Know Your Value to Understand Your Worth~

Of course, it wouldn't be a book about relationships unless we talk about knowing your worth and your value. Because I'm often told that my mind works differently than others, I will approach it from a slightly different angle than I have often seen. I believe you must first know your value to understand your worth. Often in literature, we see these terms used interchangeably, but I want to look at them as two separate parts that make up a whole.

Value can be defined as the worth of something in terms of the amount of other things for which it can be exchanged. By using this definition, we state that the value of something is determined by the worth of what it can be exchanged for. For my spiritual sprinters, I'm pretty sure you have caught on to where I'm taking this. John 3:16, the verse that everyone knows, says "for God so loved the world that He gave His only begotten Son, that those who believe in Him shall not perish, but have eternal life". If we compare this verse to the definition of value we are using above, your value has skyrocketed. If you were stock, everyone would be buying in at this point.

You are more valuable than you can even imagine since the One that owns everything cares enough about you to exchange His only Son for your life[14]. It should leave you speechless to think about how God sees you, how He cares for you, how in love He is with you. Even more astounding is that He cared this much for you even before you knew who He was! Before you were born[15], before you were saved[16], He had already orchestrated the way to reconcile you back to Himself[17]. You truly are a jewel in his crown[18].

Now that we understand value, let's talk about worth. The definition most appropriate for worth as it is used here is that it "implies an especially high spiritual quality of mind and character or moral excellence; good or important enough to justify"[19]. Let's break this apart into two different sections. The first portion of this definition states your worth is measured by your spiritual strength or moral character. Therefore, by this definition, your worth complements your value. Your value is measured by what can be given in exchange for you, but your worth tells what will be gained in the exchange. God saw your value as worthy of exchanging His Son for your ransom, but what are you worth to Him? What has He gained in this barter?

I believe to Him, our spiritual growth is more valuable than any earthly pleasure or blessing that we could

gain. He wants us to prosper as our soul prospers[20]. As a woman, 1 Peter 3:4 tells us that our gentle and quiet spirit is what is pleasing to God, not based on the outward

---

[14] 1 Timothy 2:5-6

[15] Jeremiah 1:5

[16] Romans 5:8

[17] 2 Corinthians 5:18

[18] Zechariah 9:16

[19] Dictionary.com

[20] 3 John 2

appearance. As a male, 1 Samuel 16 speaks on God judging the heart and not relying on what can be seen only by the natural eye[21]. In Psalm 1, we are told that we are blessed if we do not sit with the ungodly or walk with the unrighteous, but meditate on the Word day and night.

Several times in the Bible, it speaks of those who God called faithful or blessed because of their spiritual strength and character: Enoch was taken up without experiencing death; Abraham and Sarah were counted faithful; even the prostitute Rahab was listed amongst the Faith Hall of Fame—all because of their character (Hebrews 11). Your worth measured by God derives from what is in your heart and not how well you can dress it up on the outside. Christ will gain a Bride without spot or blemish—and for Him that was worth His sacrifice.

From a marital standpoint, Proverbs 31:10 states that a good wife is worth far above rubies, and in Proverbs 12:4 she is called a crown upon her husband's head. A man is willing to exchange his Singleness and share his worldly gains, as well as his name, with a woman in whom he finds value; she is worth giving up his single status in exchange for the favor he will gain from her. He sees the value of a Proverbs 31 woman worth the exchange. In the same token, a woman knows that a man who delights in the commands of the Lord[22] and walks in integrity[16][23] is worthy of entrusting the favor God has bestowed on her; only for her
     husband to unlock.

God also sees you as good and important enough to justify. Romans states that we are justified by grace through faith in Jesus Christ. While we were yet sinners and

[21] 1 Samuel 16:6-8

[22] Psalm 112:1

[23] Proverbs 10:9

enemies of God, He saw it fit to send His Son as an atonement for our sins. I can't think of any other expression that could compare to how much your value was worth everything to God. Because He values us, we live this spiritual walk for Him so we can lay the very crowns He has given us at His feet, showing Him that He is worth it all to us, as well. No one wants to be in love alone, including God. Because God cannot lie and He has loved us with an everlasting love[24], it is our reasonable service to return our love to Him with our lives[25].

Our justification is found all throughout Romans. We are justified by faith in Christ. Therefore, our worth comes from accepting the value that He has bestowed on us, allowing His character to give back to Him the very things that He has deposited in us.

~Diminished Value~

Now that we have explored the difference between our value, our worth, and how God sees us, we can look at it from the natural sense in relationships. What happens when our value is diminished? Can this even happen? I don't believe so.

Not too long ago, our Singles ministry hosted a Singles Brunch. As one of the icebreakers, we played the "Penny Game." Everyone was given a penny and instructed to recant something interesting that happened to them in the year on the penny. As I was passing out the pennies, someone made a comment that their penny was rusty, and they asked to trade it for a new, shiny one. At that moment

---

[24] Jeremiah 31:3
[25] Romans 12:1

God dropped into my spirit, "Just because it's rusty doesn't make it any less valuable. It just needs to be cleaned up."

You may be this penny. You may have to work a little bit harder or dig a bit deeper to uncover the value, but it's still there waiting to be rediscovered. Just like this young lady who forgot the value of her penny because of the rust, many people can't see your value because you are covered in "gunk". Some of it derives from self-inflicted pain because of relationships, disobedience, and sin. Others may have imposed some of it on you through abuse, neglect, or molestation. Whatever the source, it causes people to miss your true value because they can't see the clean copy.

Thanks be to God, that He doesn't see the gunk but recognizes our true value; He sees the Blood of Jesus. All we need to do is be soaked in the alcohol of the Word[26]. Although your value was always there, it can now be seen by the naked eye. Remember your value can never be diminished because God states your worth trading His Son's life for yours, and no amount of gunk can cover that up.

I am reminded of the story of the adulterous wife in Hosea. God continued to tell Hosea to go back to get his wife. As many times as she left him, he was instructed to go back and retrieve her[27]. This book shows a direct relationship with God and His chosen people, showing us that as long as we return to Him, He will always return to us[28].

The Prodigal Son is another story about perceived tarnished value. The son was at the end of his rope and planned to go back to offer himself as a servant to his

---

[26] Psalm 51:2,7

[27] Hosea 3:1

[28] Hosea 12:6

father, because he believed that his value as a son had been diminished. But what happened? While he was still a far way off, his father ran to him, kissed him and clothed him back into his birthright. This is an amazing story of redemption. It illustrates that in God's eyes, we are seen the way He created us and not by the things of the world we have allowed to define or defile us. Because He has sealed us with His Spirit and we are now in covenant with Him[29], He is not swayed by how "dirty" we have become in the world. He is waiting to make our scarlet sins white as snow[30]. Our Father's love is truly amazing.

The struggle we often face is coming back to our right mind like the Prodigal Son and asking our Father to take us back. But I assure you, just as his father welcomed him before he could say a word, your heavenly Father stands at the door and knocks waiting to wash you in His Word[31]. Will you answer? Speak over yourself what your Father spoke in the beginning. Habakkuk 3:17 states He will rejoice over you with singing. You don't need a new penny. You just need your shine restored.

~Still on the Tree~

So, what about those of you that understand your value and worth in Christ and your penny is in mint condition, shiny and new, yet your desire for marriage has not been actualized? In fact, it's the opposite. It seems like everyone is being chosen but you. You may be asking yourself, "How did I get here? Has God forgotten me? What is wrong with me?"

---

[29] Ephesians 1:11-14
[30] Isaiah 1:18
[31] Ephesians 5:26

This is a dangerous cycle to get caught in. You will soon be sucked into the green-eyed monster and start comparing

yourself to those very people that you call friends. Rest assured, because the devil loves mess and messy people, when you do this, he will always make the scales tip in your favor in the "marriage-material" category.

You will begin to believe that you are more worthy to be married than the other person. Remember Paul warned against this type of boasting in 2 Corinthians 11. When we start to focus on our accomplishments, and how good or "holy" we are, the enemy has succeeded in convincing us to count on our resources rather than our Source.

This trick is literally as old as time, yet it is still working. Remember the enemy is not always looking to take you out, especially if you are saved, because even he understands to be absent in the body is to be present with the Lord[32]. You are more useful to him if you are ineffective. You become one of his prized possessions when you can cause someone else to stumble. Comparisons are a dangerous game to play because spiritually, you are telling God that you don't approve of His plan for your life and that you would rather have someone else's.

So, here you are still on the tree, always being passed up while the apples that are on the ground or on the lower branches are being picked so easily; seemingly without even trying. Now doubt is setting in. As a woman, you start to wonder, "Am I not pretty enough? Is there something wrong with me? Do I not have the right body type or skin tone?" As a man, you may start to believe, "I'm not accomplished enough. I don't have the right education. I'm too nice. I mean, no one really wants a coming-up brother

---

[32] 2 Corinthians 5:8

anymore, huh?" Change your perspective; you are approaching this all wrong.

I have heard a popular saying that states, "Women are like apples on trees. The best ones are at the top of the tree. Some men don't want to reach for the good ones because they are afraid of falling and getting hurt (or even worse, having to put out actual effort to get you). Instead, they pick the ones on the ground, which are easier. The apples at the top may begin to think there is something wrong with them. But no, you are amazing! You just have to wait for the right man that realizes you're worth the climb" (and will ask God for the ladder).

I believe the truth is not that the apples which have gotten picked are better than you (or less than you, for that matter). It's simply that God saw fit that it was their time. The reason they were picked may be that God knew the one meant to pick them was on the way. They may have been in the same position you are in: at the top of the tree, seemingly forgotten, asking the same questions you are asking, questioning their value. I encourage you to keep waiting. Whether God supplies a ladder or bends the branches, you will be just in the reach of the one God has chosen when he comes.

Maybe you are still on the tree because you aren't quite ripe yet. Stay there for a while. Mature on the Vine as you grow stronger[33]. When it's your time, there is no way that you will get passed over. Remember the view is better from the top. Use it to your advantage to weed out those who aren't strong enough to make it to the top to get you.

~Truly Complete~

---

[33] John 15:4-5

"Complete in Christ" may sound cliché, but that doesn't make it any less true. There is no way that you can complement the one that God has for you until you allow God to complete you. There is a God-sized hole in you that only He can fill. Because He gives us free will, He will patiently wait for us to try to fit other things into it: a career, a car, a relationship, or a degree, only to realize that we are still empty inside. There will always be a lack because we were created in His image to be used for His purpose. You were created for God's pleasure, not your own.

Let's discuss understanding your purpose in context with His plan. If we stop looking at Singleness as something to get out of, but as something to really get into, our perspective on waiting for our mate will drastically change.

~3

Getting In Before You Get Out

"The thief does not come except to steal, and to kill, and to destroy. I have come that they may have life, and that they may have it more abundantly"
~ John 10:10, NKJV

When we are unable to find tranquility within ourselves, it is useless to seek it elsewhere.
~Francois de la Rochefoucauld

So what does the term "get in before you get out" mean? It directly relates to your mindset and your perspective. God has placed us in Singleness for a reason and He has a direct plan associated with this time in our lives. He means for us to accomplish everything that He has planned for us in this season before He moves us to the next.

Think naturally of a cake that is baking. Grandma always says don't open the oven before it's ready. If you had a Madea like me, she would even say jumping or walking too hard in the area would make the cake fall. If we take this process into our spiritual imagination, I believe that it relates to our Singleness. Coming out of it too soon, or having outside factors hinder our full development in this area, is equivalent to getting out before we get in. If you have ever had a cake that fell in the oven or didn't cook all the way through, you will remember it being gooey in the middle and you had to eat around the edges. You may have had to toss the entire cake and start over again. Your Singleness can be likened to this scenario. God wants your Singleness to develop completely so that He can use every part for His glory. Stay in the oven until His timer goes off.

~Intent for Singleness~

There are many specific intentions for your Singleness, and these will be discovered as you turn over your desires and plans to God and allow Him to replace them with His desires for you. He will reveal His established plans to you as you spend time with Him. Some will be directly in line with those that we will discuss in this book and some will be catered to your individual walk. Ask God what He specifically intends for you in this season and when He reveals it, have the courage to act.

There are some general intentions that I believe God has for all Singles in their Single season. This is by no means an exhaustive list, nor will each category highlight God's specific plan for your time alone with Him. Through discernment and prayer, God will reveal His specific plan for you, so be open to what He is speaking to your heart.

Why am I still Single? If you are anything like me and the millions of other Singles out there, you have asked yourself this question and even screamed it at God numerous times. And not unlike me, you may have been met with a deafening silence. God has now changed my viewpoint on what I perceived as silence, and opened my heart to understanding Singleness the way He designed it.

God views Singleness as a time of undistracted devotion unto the Lord; a time that the Lover of your soul can romance and woo you. This is a time that the Redeemer of our souls pursues and overtakes us with a love so pure and so sweet it compares with nothing else, because we will never experience anything else like it. Who wouldn't want to prolong that?

This is a time that God has set apart for you to work wholeheartedly for His kingdom without the distractions of earthly responsibilities like a mate and family. Once you have allowed your heart to be saturated with this kind of love, I believe your mindset will no longer be, "I 'have' to get through this season," but rather, "I 'get' to experience this season!" You will truly learn to enjoy it. If marriage is in His will, there may be a significant adjustment period in learning to put all the distractions away to get some time alone with Him like this again. So take full advantage of this time as it was intended and get drenched in His love.

Another purpose for Singleness is to focus on defining yourself. Many times when we talk about getting ourselves together before marriage, we focus on finances, credit scores and other material things. While I do believe that these things are important I believe if we focus on getting our internal right, then the external will begin to line up. A good name is more desirable than great riches[34]. When we allow God to line up our character with what He has already defined for us, then the natural will line up with the spiritual.

The Lord's Prayer says, "Thy kingdom come, Thy will be done, on earth as it is in Heaven." I'm just now fully grasping what this verse means in my Single life. His will for me has already been predestined and orchestrated in Heaven, so when I pray this prayer I am commanding my natural man to line up with what my spiritual man already is.

But a word of caution: be very careful of what you pray for because when you pray petitions from your mouth, you give them permission to line up and manifest. Prayer is serious, and can mean life or death to many situations in your life[35]. Because God loves us so much, He will answer "no" to protect us from casual and callous prayers prayed only from our finite perspective. I'm grateful that we serve a God that is not moved by our prayers more than His ordained purpose. What we desire will never take precedence over what He has planned. I praise Him daily for unanswered and denied prayers. I can't tell you how many times I prayed, "God please let him be the one, but

---

[34] Proverbs 22:1

[35] Proverbs 18:21

not my will but Yours, but please God I really want him to be the one." How foolish was I to believe that persuasive verbiage, could somehow manipulate God into giving me my desires, instead of fulfilling His will. Remind you of a certain story involving a talking donkey?

In Numbers 22, Balaam prays to God for his own selfish purposes and God answers no. Being that God already knew Balaam's heart, He allowed him to go, but only after giving him very specific instructions. As Balaam was going, God's wrath burned towards him and his motives and He sent an angel to kill Balaam. Can you relate? When God says no, do you accept it as final, or do you try to engineer your prayers to get a yes, by any means necessary?

God later showed Balaam mercy and directed his steps even in his disobedience. Needless to say—I'm glad that God doesn't concede and give me everything that I impulsively pray for. There is no way that our mediocre minds or thoughts could ever imagine what God has planned for us. Prayerfully, our requests will change and we will begin to mean and fully understand what it means to pray, "Nevertheless, not my will, God but Yours be done." God intends for this season to be an opportunity to learn to pray as Christ does, for His will to come to earth.

~Sheep lead by His Voice~

Have you ever been in a crowd full of people, talking and enjoying yourself, not really focusing on what was going on around you and then you hear your name mentioned in another conversation across the room? You immediately get distracted and tune into what that person is saying. Why is this?

In Neuroscience, there is a concept called the Cocktail Party Phenomenon, which states that our brains have a way of drowning out background and irrelevant noises to allow us to focus on the conversation that we are participating in. In the same way, we will localize our attention to our name because we recognize it as something we naturally orient to from our personal investment in it. We have become so accustomed and attuned to the sound of our own name it can break our attention away from the deepest of conversations to focus across the room. We are personally invested in whatever our name is associated with, so we tune in to it, as a protective mechanism to make sure that we are not being defamed or misrepresented, but also because we have been programmed to respond when it is called.

Spiritually, I believe God wants us to use our Singleness to do the same with His voice and His name. He wants us to use this time of minimal distractions to fine tune our ear to His voice. We should become so attuned to His voice, His commands, and His direction that it breaks into whatever else we are doing and demands our attention. We should use our Singleness as a time to understand His voice and practice listening for His direction, so when we are in the "cocktail party" of life, marriage, and career we can pick it out as easy as our own name being called.

Divine guidance only comes to prepared hearts. If you have not spent the time preparing and waiting for the guidance, you will not recognize it when it comes. You may even take matters into your own hands because you don't understand how to wait until He speaks. Sharpen your ears to hear the words of the Lord. When we are in tune with Him, as sheep led by a shepherd, we won't have to doubt that He has spoken because we recognize His voice[36]. Being in tune with His voice also gives us protection from strangers because if we are tempted or we are being lead into something that is contrary to what we know He sounds like (regarding His character and direction), then we will be able to withstand and not be so easily lead astray. You hear that which you are more attuned to listen for. Learn His voice at this time and when you hear it, follow its direction.

Singleness is not where we just happen to be; it is where God has divinely placed us. If God put you here then there is no way that He can forget or overlook you. You are not His car keys or His glasses. You are the precious jewel in His crown, the heir of His righteousness, worth trading the value of His Son in exchange. He's got you. Seeking to understand His character during this time will make it a lot easier to know who you are to Him because you truly understand who He is to you.

~Satisfied and Content~

---

[36] John 10:27

So now that you have committed to getting to know Christ in this period and letting Him woo you to experience that everlasting love, it's time to face one of the most challenging components of this walk. I believe that knowing God is not the most difficult part of our Singleness. In fact, His Word says in Jeremiah 29 that if we seek Him with our whole hearts then we shall find Him. Because we have established that this Single time is meant to be free of worldly distractions, we are free to focus our whole being on seeking a findable God. Finding a balance between being satisfied and seeking contentment, is where the challenge lies.

In our Singles ministry, we often discussed the difference between being content and satisfied in our Singleness. Many times these words are used interchangeably, but there is a slight difference that I wish to highlight. Being content is defined as desiring no more than what we have, assenting to, or willing to accept the circumstances[37].

By definition, this takes the responsibility of getting anything out of our Singleness off us and states that it is almost something that is uncontrollable. Therefore, by hiding behind this definition, we have no choice but to accept whatever it brings. Now the definition for satisfied is being filled with satisfaction or paid or discharged in full as a debt. This opens up a completely new possibility. This now takes the responsibility of our Singleness into our own

---

[37] Dictionary.com

hands and states that we have a choice to come out of it full.

We will be discharged out of our Singleness into marriage when God sees fit and in His will, but what we do while here becomes our choice. We can meander through this time and be content or we can choose to ride this thing until the wheels fall off and come out of Singleness full and satisfied—not experiencing the "if I would have known then what I know now" situations. It's your choice and your decision, but I'm sure you can guess which one God desires for you.

~To Thine Own Self be True~

I think that another difficult part comes when we seek to understand ourselves in this time. As you understand this stage in your life, really get to know yourself while you are Single. Like, really. Figure out the good, the bad, and the ugly about yourself. It's hard to tell someone else what you're not going to put up with when you don't know what they have to put up with from you.

This is the time to build your personal resume of sorts, with your accomplishments, shortcomings, fears, desires, etc. What are your quirks? Your deal breakers? Do you really know yourself, like the innermost parts? If someone were to ask you to describe yourself in 10 words, what would come to mind? The majority of us would only be able to come up with four to five words before we start talking about what we have, or what we do, instead of who we truly are. We define ourselves by our job, house, cars, ministry positions and other things, but yet we don't really know who we are as a person. What you do and who you are—two vastly different things. Use this time to understand that difference. Begin to define yourself by God's standards of what He says about you instead of what the world tells you. You are fearfully and wonderfully made. God designed you before you were conceived, before you were formed in your mother's womb and He called you before you were born[38]. This alone bestows a distinct awe for who you were created to be. Allow God to shatter the image that the world has tricked you into believing and restore the shine of your copper penny.

To thine own self be true. I believe that Shakespeare had divine revelation when he wrote this line. Whether we translate it into the current usage of knowing ourselves and being faithful to that, or by Polonius' definition to look out for our own best interests and being true to the person we are, they both hold very relevant truths. If we don't know ourselves then there is no way we can be true. Singleness is a time to get to know self. The real you—not the one that everyone sees, or your representative that you send on dates and interviews, but the "you" that you go to bed with at night. This is who you need to get to know and understand before you add the task of knowing your mate.

~Take Advantage of This Time~

---

[38] Jeremiah 1:4-5

Use this time to fix whatever you are not happy about in your life, because it won't magically get better in marriage. In fact, it will get worse because you have now brought a "Single" problem into your "married" relationship. If you are a selfish, immature, insecure, sexually frustrated Single, you will still have these struggles when you get married until you allow God to heal these areas. Sweeping them under the rug or thinking that they will disappear once you get married is delusional and could be detrimental to building a healthy

partnership. You will now have to focus on situations that could have and should have been fixed in the Single stage of your life as a married individual. You will end up draining the one you are with, attempting to seek a healing that can only be provided by God.

Build that personal resume; the list of what you will

bring to the table. From a woman's perspective, many times we are so quick to tell a person what we expect and what we are not going to do in a dating relationship that we fail to mention what we will do. What do we have to offer that will make this person want to make a concentrated effort in sharing in our life? If you can't quickly and surely answer that question, that may be another task to accomplish in your Single life.

Naturally speaking, would you buy a car if the dealer's only sales pitch was, "This car doesn't go over 100MPH, it doesn't turn sharp corners very well, it requires you to change the oil and filter every other month, and requires you to change the brakes yearly with monthly scheduled maintenance. It is oversized so you will have to find special parking for it, and after 50,000 miles, what you see is what you get because the warranty expires." I can pretty much guarantee that you would hesitate in buying it because nothing was explained in an attractive manner. Although all of the mentioned is true to the car, it is not what you lead with if you want to make a sell. I believe to an extent, the same concept applies with relationships. If all the person is informed of is the effort they are required to put in, and they are not presented with any of the perks of how you will add value to their life, or what distinguishes you from all the others; it may be a bit more difficult to get them to buy in. This should not be misconstrued to say that all of the "maintenance" shouldn't be addressed, because you definitely don't want to make my mistake of portraying the "perfect mate' from Chapter 2. Discuss them, but don't blow your own sale with the wrong pitch.

While you're Single, use this time to beef up your resume. Finish school, start your business, pay off your debt and make your resume speak for itself. Become your best you. Figure out your sales pitch. God has His best companion orchestrated for you, but I don't believe that He will ordain that appointment until you are working to be your best. You can't expect to get a ten if you are slumming it around the fives.

Date yourself. The same energy that you would spend getting to know the ins and outs of a potential boo, use that time getting to know yourself. Find out your quirks, your fears, your hopes, your deal-breakers, and your annoying habits (no, you are not perfect); even what type of eggs you like in the morning. You would be surprised how much stuff about you that you don't even know. Might sound silly, but this encounter with self can be powerful—if done right.

I spent time going to restaurants alone and ordering dinner. This may be a small feat for you, but for me it was a big one. I am always the last person to order at the table. I am that one who asks everyone else what I should eat, that one who ends up getting six suggestions from the wait staff, only to order something totally different. Doesn't bother me, but I've seen some people get pretty annoyed by it. Upon marriage, I will freely turn over to my husband this task. Let's just call it an added perk to being the head of the household.

I've also learned that although I love to visit other places, I don't have a burning desire to live outside of Texas. I almost always overdress for an event. I can't do cold weather well. I think matching is overrated and cats and lizards scare me. These are only a few of my quirks; you would be wise to figure out yours while you only have yours to worry about.

Marriage is not a be-all-end-all-cure-all to the issues that you face as a Single. Whatever issues you have now, you will have them married, unless you take care of them beforehand. It's one thing to be incomplete and miserable Single, but it's a whole 'nother thing to be that and be going to bed with someone else every night.

A minister once said that during marital counseling, a vast majority of the problems he encountered with couples were "Single" problems and not "married" issues. He elaborated that examples of Single problems are bad credit, poor financial planning, no direction in life, excessive shopping habits, low self-esteem, or image issues. Married problems are squeezing the toothpaste from the middle or the bottom, washing the dishes at night or in the morning, or taking off clothes and leaving a trail to the bedroom after work. He believes that the majority of marital counseling issues are derived from single problems that either one or both parties didn't deal with while they were Single, and brought into the marriage. Fix whatever is lacking or needs improvement in your Single life in order to not bring it into your marriage.

If you are lonely, there is a reason for that. What is it about yourself that makes being alone uncomfortable? Remember the difference in being lonely and alone. The two are not synonymous and do not have to co-exist. You can't be alone (although you can feel alone) in the presence of others, but you can be lonely in a crowd full of people. I consider being alone and content an art. It is not something many people can claim that they do well. Learn to enjoy it now as a Single, so that when you get those moments married, you will remember how precious they really are.

I've spoken to married people that disclosed how they felt lonely in their marriage and I can only imagine the heartache this brings. I was never alone in my engagement per se, but I was desperately lonely. I now realize the value of respecting my time alone and the seriousness of cohabitation in marriage because we can't say, "Go home please," or "I would like to be alone now," to our spouse without one person being uprooted from their own home. Your space is no longer your own, so being confined with a person that leaves you feeling lonely (or desperately making you wish you were alone) should spark another sober examination of your readiness for marriage.

One strategy of learning the art of being alone but not feeling lonely is to practice being by yourself. Turn the TV off, cut off your ringer, sign off from Facebook and Twitter, and just be. Commit to not filling the silence, but to embrace it and just rest in the peace of being with you. It's easier said than done. The average person can only comfortably stand silence for a few seconds when in the presence of other people without trying to fill it in some way. I have lived alone for the past nine years and I have only recently begun to understand the magnitude of being content alone, and I still find it hard to just be and really do nothing. When I am alone, I am either reading a book, watching a movie, talking on the phone, cleaning the house, or doing something else. It is almost unnatural just to do nothing. Why is this? I believe partially because we seek companionship; we were created to be together.

Christ exemplifies this concept when He states that we are many members but one body[39] and the Bible even advises against being alone because there is no one to help us up when we fall[40]. Although God understands the desire

---

[39] Romans 12:5

and need for companionship, (because He created it) I don't believe that He was saying to never be alone. Jesus would often steal away to be alone with our Father[41]. Desiring company or the pleasure of being with others is not to be seen as negative, but it can be a crutch if you don't know how to be comfortable alone. At this point in your life, you have the choice to spend as much time alone as you desire and I encourage you to enjoy it fully—soak it all in. When you get married, your space will be shared with your mate and your family, so this will turn into one of those, "If I would have known then what I know now" moments. Time to be alone then may be a rare commodity.

~You Could Be Married~

You could be married right now. Do you believe this? Everyone could be married if they wanted to be, so why are you not? Everyone could find someone to marry them, but for some reason you aren't married. I believe that if you went through your mental black book, you would run across at least one person that wanted to marry you at some point or that you desired to marry. If we are honest, there is probably still someone out there that would be willing to marry us right now.

It's not hard at all to find a spouse, but for some reason you decided not to marry whether it was a distinct, conscious decision or an unconscious standard to not settle

---

[40] Ecclesiastes 4:10
[41] Luke 6:12, Mark 1:35, Luke 5:16

for someone who wasn't designed for you. You decided to wait not for whom you could have, but for whom you should have. I believe that a standard has been set in your mind that you will not settle to be married for the sake of being married, but that you will wait for the glorious union that God has already coordinated in the heavens.

Hence, that means you chose Singleness. Now that puts a completely different spin on it. If we revisit our discussion on the difference between being content and satisfied, now we can recognize that not only is our choice of how we perceive Singleness up to us, but the very decision to be Single is in our hands as well. Therefore, we must now take full responsibility for our Singleness and what we do with it because it was (and still is) a direct choice of our free will.

Blows your mind to think of it this way, huh? I know, because it continues to perplex me, but I use this as a reality check when I begin to question God as to why I'm not married yet. It's not only a decision that we made once, but a decision that we daily renew when we decide not to settle for less than what God's will is for us.

~Singleness is a Talent~

Many Singles are afraid to accept their calling in Singleness because they are petrified that God will look down, see them happy, and then decide that they don't need to be married. I believed this myself, so I did everything possible to ensure God knew I was unhappy in this state so He would hurry up and get me out of it.

This is another trick of the enemy—don't believe it! If we give this mindset a dose of reality and take off the clouded goggles we are looking through, we can easily see this concept doesn't even make sense. How can we believe that if we decide to enjoy a gift we will never receive another?

Go with me to Matthew 25, the Parable of the Talents. In this illustration, the Master gives each servant talents according to their own abilities without instructions as to what to do with them. I believe He trusted them to rely on what they knew about His character to guide them in what to do with each talent. Each servant acted according to how they perceived their Master. (This point is very important so remember it, because we will come back to it.)

As the parable develops, the servant that was given five talents invested them and gained five more; the servant given two-doubled his investment as well, but then we arrive at the servant who was given one talent. He decided to do nothing with his talent, in fact, he decided to bury it so he could give back exactly what he received. I can't presume to understand his mindset or what lead him to believe that his Master would be OK with just receiving back the original talent, but as we read on, the servant states he knew the Master was a hard man and acted in fear. He was rebuked and his talent was taken from him and given to the servant that restored back to the Master more than he had originally been given.

What do we take away from this story? There are two portions of this passage that directly relates to our Singleness. The first is that each received talents according to their own abilities. If we combine this story with the analogy of the gifts in Chapter 2, we can see that the Master bestowed different gifts on each servant in line with what he could handle. I don't believe it to be coincidental that the servant who buried his talent was only given one talent to begin with. If we understand the talents were given according to their abilities, this speaks to the fact that this servant had not shown himself as being wise or a good steward in the first place, because the Master already knew he could only be trusted with one. I would go so far as to say that even being given the one talent was an act of faith on the Master's part—a second, third or maybe even another chance to prove his abilities in an area that he had fallen short in before.

Do you see the parallel to your Single life? If God can trust us with our Single life, to invest it and give Him back more than what He originally gave us, then why would we let the enemy tell us God wouldn't give us more? I believe enjoying our life and truly using it for God's glory is showing ourselves to be worthy of receiving more talents and entering into His rest, when He returns. Use your Singleness to the fullest to show you can be trusted to use your married life in the same fashion, when the time is appointed.

The second takeaway from this passage for Singleness is the perception of the Master. The unwise servant believed that the Master was a hard man, so therefore only wanted to claim what belonged to Him. He was afraid to take a risk for fear that he would lose and upset the Master, so he settled for just returning exactly what he had received. This view was distorted, but his perception was his reality and it affected how he treated what he received from the Master. I think this directly relates to our view of God. If we spend the time getting to know His character and becoming attuned to His voice as we discussed earlier, we will be able to discern His good and pleasing will[42]. I believe it is safe to say that the servant with the one talent didn't know his Master; he only knew of Him. There is a big difference between the two. If he had taken the time to glean from the Master, he would have been wise and privy to the motives and mindset He exemplified.

So the question now becomes, "Do you know God or do you only know of Him?" John 1 states that as many as received Him, He gave them the right to be called sons of God. Then continuing in that same book, Chapter 15 states we are no longer called servants, but friends of God because we have access to everything that God has made

---

[42] Romans 12:2

known to Christ, our Master. I believe if we really knew Him, there is no way anyone could convince us that He would do anything that was not in line with His character. The only way we would doubt that He could withhold any good thing from us, is if we didn't really know Him. I

challenge you to really get to know Him, so that the washing of His Word will remove all those doubts, allowing His perfect love to cast out all fear[43].

If you believe that God will supply all of your needs according to His riches and you're still Single, then that's probably Him supplying your needs at this time. The Father gives good things to His children[44]; when you doubt His hand it's because you don't truly know His face.

In the book of Jeremiah, Chapter 29, we usually beeline straight to verse 11 while ignoring the rest of the chapter. Take some time, read it again, and try focusing on the entire passage in context. God is speaking through Jeremiah to the Israelites while they are in exile in Babylon. Many of them were putting their lives on hold waiting on God to deliver them. Can you imagine their shock when He told them to get comfortable and put down their roots[45]? God is telling you the same thing. Get comfortable in this status and when the established time for you to be brought out comes, He will bring you out. And because you were obedient in prospering while you were in

---

[43] 1 John 4:18
[44] James 1:17
[45] Jeremiah 29:4-7

an "uncomfortable" situation, you will come out with more than with which you entered.

~Uncover the Value~

Going back to the illustration of the penny, sometimes our Singleness' value is hidden. It may be covered by others' images and ideas of what Singleness is or what we have been told it is supposed to be. How many times in your daily life do you see a penny on the street and look over it continuing to walk, thinking "It's just a penny"?

As Single people, we may feel this way at times; passed over and not picked because we aren't presumed to be "valuable" enough. We think metaphorically, "If I were a quarter someone would pick me up." The moment we begin to think this way is the moment doubt takes root in our lives. Doubt that we are missing something or that our current position isn't important enough. Be careful because that's the same lie the enemy convinced Eve to believe. She began to think that the plan she was carrying out in her life was lacking something and the God who loved her was the one holding out.

This view can be combated by changing your perspective. For someone, that penny (your penny) is what makes them a dollar. You are the perfect match for someone and some purpose. It may take 100 pennies to make a dollar, but what you need to know is that although it may take time, your Singleness will add up. Give it the opportunity for its value to appreciate.

One of my favorite verses is Matthew 11:28-30 (MSG) which reads:

"Are you tired? Worn out? Burned out on religion? Come to Me. Get away with Me and you'll recover your life. I'll show you how to take a real rest. Walk with Me and work with Me— watch how I do it. Learn the unforced rhythms of grace. I won't lay anything heavy or ill-fitting on you. Keep company with Me and you'll learn to live freely and lightly."

Simply powerful. When you get tired of the world telling you about your God, your Singleness, and what you should be doing, prayerfully you will steal away with God and allow Him to refresh you. Let Him and only Him define your Singleness and truly learn to live freely and lightly.

~Keeping Marriage in the Proper Perspective~

Marriage has to stay in its proper perspective. You become a defeated Christian Single when you spend so much time being preoccupied with getting married, that you become ineffective in your Singleness. Don't get so caught up in the bondage of married-mindedness that you miss the freedom of Singleness. A special freedom comes from having only to think on the things of the Lord right now. We lose that when we start dwelling on, "When I get married, I will…" or "My husband and I will…"

NewsFlash! While you are busy planning your future, you are failing to live in your present! You are telling God the stage you are in isn't worthy enough for you to actualize or develop, so you will just bury it and wait on Him to return to get you out of it. This same viewpoint comes from only knowing of the Master and His plan, instead of investing the effort of really getting to know Him. I caution you to remember what happened to the unwise servant with this same viewpoint.

We have to use our Single season to learn how to fit our lives around our time with God, not fitting God around our lives. In the first scenario, our agenda and plans are on the throne of our heart; in the latter, Christ is. Singleness is a time to anchor, deadbolt, and superglue Christ to the top priority in our life because if He is not on the throne as a Single, He will not magically jump on it when we get married. The purpose of our Singleness is to be used for God's glory. If He is not getting glory from our Single life, how can we imagine Him getting it from our married life? Jeremiah 29:11 says God knows the plans He has for us, of good and not of evil, to give us a hope and an expected end. So, our Singleness is in His plan just as our marriage will be. If marriage is the "expected end" to this stage of our life, why not enjoy the journey getting there?

It's been stated that a Single person once said, "I hope Jesus doesn't come back before I get married." Although maybe spoken in jest, it's sad because many of us agree with this. We can't allow earthly pleasures to take precedence over an eternal perspective. That you would even consider prolonging being in this world, in exchange for your heavenly home, shows signs of a deeper issue. Anything more important than being with your Heavenly King has become an idol—even marriage.

Once marriage becomes an idol the enemy has succeeded in distracting us, and a distracted Christian is an ineffective Christian. If you focus so much on the one tree that you can't have, Eve, you will forget about every other tree that is at your disposal. I believe this is how she was lured away, by her own lust for what was forbidden. Satan convinced her that the only thing that she didn't have was the one thing she couldn't live without. He is still using the same trick on us today. Why? Because it is still working. He doesn't have to change his M.O. because we are still falling for it. If he can get us to doubt God's love and provision by making us feel like He is withholding something good, then he can get us to doubt everything else our faith has already proven[46].

Satan's goal is not only to kill you. To kill you would only push you into the arms of your Creator. That wouldn't benefit him at all and you are much more valuable to him being ineffective. An ineffective Christian is one that will get to Heaven, but won't bring anyone else with him. One who is not growing in God, not performing His will, and not working for the Kingdom. Now this Christian—Satan can use. You are more valuable to him than a legion of his demons at this point. Because no one will expect you to be used by him, he can slip you in under the radar and

---

[46] 2 Corinthians 11:2-3

infiltrate places that his demons would be recognized. Because you are so depressed in your Single state, you miss the wonderful blessings of this season and end up pulling down everyone connected to you. Don't be the devil's punk. Fight for your contentment and remember who you are and Whose you are.

~It Has its Advantages~

There are so many advantages of being Single; discover them. There are many things that you can do and should be doing while you are Single and if you take your eyes off the anticipation of marriage for a moment, maybe you would see them.

There are numerous highlights to this Single life. Single, you can lay spread eagle across your king-size bed and not worry about sharing the covers. Single, you don't have to cook if you don't want to—Diet Dr. Pepper and gummy bears are equivalent to steak and potatoes if you are tired enough. Pack up, go on a weeklong trip (if you have the liberties), and don't tell anyone but Mom for emergency reasons; you have the freedom not to have to check in. Use it.

When we get married we will have a curfew—and yes, we should want one. Why would you even consider staying out all the time when you recognize what you have at home? Enjoy your solitude while you still have it. Ladies, watch a romantic comedy marathon all day. Gentleman, play Madden until the sun comes back up, or vice versa.

The beauty of living alone is no one will have to know unless you tell them. And your secret is safe with me.

Furthermore, this is the only time that we can make decisions based solely on God and ourselves. Don't wait to do something, go somewhere or buy anything, because the spouse may not approve when they arrive. I have spoken to many Single people who were putting off a task, or afraid to take a risk, for fear of what their future spouse would say or think. I used to be this person until I realized how ridiculous this was. My husband is not here! I am Single! May sound basic, but a lot of Singles struggle with making decisions based on now, and not what they anticipate. I was even told not to cut my hair because my husband may not like short hair. My response, "Well, he better start growing his now." It took me too long to realize that my life only belongs to Christ at this point, and He doesn't care if my hair is long or short or whether my clothes match—as long as I'm being effective for His kingdom. Remember, tomorrow is not promised, and it has enough troubles of its own. Finding the balance means not being so focused on the destination that you miss the enjoyment of the journey.

Rest assured, God will not instruct you to move to Africa if your husband is in America (unless it's temporary or He has a plan to move him there as well). I have seen this happen, so I don't doubt that God can still orchestrate the direction of my Single life to line up with the direction of my marriage, and it's not contingent upon whether I decide to buy a town house or go back to school right now.

Allow God to direct your path at this time, He longs to show you the way. Fulfillment is in the love affair with the Lover of your soul, and He's waiting for you—are you ready?

~4

Seeking Contentment: Enjoying the Love Affair

"The Lord appeared to us from afar saying, 'I have loved you with an everlasting love; I have drawn you with unfailing kindness.'"
~Jeremiah 31:3 NIV

God loves each of us as if there were only one of us
~St. Augustine

In my biased opinion, this chapter is one of the most important in the entire book. It's shorter than some of the others because our intimate relationship with God is so individualized it would be impossible for me to tell you

how to live your walk with the Lord. But it is one of the most important because if you don't figure it out, the rest of this book is pointless.

Our relationship with Christ has to be the center of everything we do, especially our Singleness. If He is not the focus point for this season in our life, then we are assured to get dizzy and tossed around in the whirlwind of life. If singleness is supposed to be about undistracted devotion to God, and you're not using it for that purpose, then you've missed the mark. You are short-changing yourself if you don't take this time to get to know you in light of what God says about you.

If this were a dating relationship, this time would be the courtship—the time that you have decided you want to spend the rest of your lives together and you are investing time and energy in getting to know each other. Devote the same fervor you would in a potential mate, in Christ. I can tell you from experience, no one can love you better. I have truly searched all over and couldn't find anybody greater than Him. If we stop looking at Singleness as something to get out of, but as something to really understand and get into, our perspective on waiting for our mate will change.

~Contentment is a Journey Not a Destination~

This concept is very important to remember when you aren't feeling like this season is a love affair. Understanding that this truly is a journey will keep you encouraged when those broken days come. I have had several of such days. Those days I was literally screaming, rolling on the floor, crying my heart out to God and pleading for Him to release me from this hell that He was punishing me with.

I had such a day recently. While helping my sister with her wedding arrangements, I had two friends get engaged the same week and then received two wedding invitations when I checked the mail on the way home. As I walked through the front door, the last straw was made apparent when another friend's text message was received announcing her engagement!

It started with one tear…then before I realized it, I was sobbing uncontrollably and slipped down to the floor. Immobilized. This surprised me because I couldn't understand why I was crying. It wasn't jealousy because I was truly happy for my sister and all of my friends, but this day made me extremely aware of the fact that when I turned the key, no one was there waiting for me. I had to realize that although I was content being Single, I was still in this journey. I now understand that these "bad" days are natural, and even healthy to a certain extent.

I would be remiss if I wrote this book and pretended like this is not a very real, very sensitive part in our journey. Everyone will have that bad day; that day that although you are satisfied with God, your desire for marriage takes over, and then it's a struggle to regain your contentment. The key is not to stay there. The success comes when we use it as an experience to grow closer to God, not allowing the intended tactic of the devil to make us believe that God is withholding good from us.

An elder at my church coined the term, "Don't doubt in the dark what God has told you in the light." Remember that your Daddy knows what you need and these days come to remind us we still need Him in every aspect of our lives. His faithfulness is tried and true. Brokenness leads us into His arms and gives us the opportunity to lie on His chest and have Him sing over us. Acknowledge Him as Lord, but don't forget the Comforter that He is too.

So what happens if we consciously decide not to come out of this state? What if we are content in being discontent? What transpires if we decide that we don't agree with this stage in our life; the timing, the place, or anything associated with it? What if we decide we will just "wait it out" in our discontentment until God realizes that we are unhappy and allows us to pass into marriage? Maybe you should realize you can't outwait God because He exists outside of time. Although God acknowledges our free will, remember that He gave it to us and our destinies are already predetermined. He already knows what the ending will be, before we even see the beginning.

It doesn't really matter how much we complain or gripe or whine about an assignment, we still have to carry it out. If it is ordained, we will go through it. God is not a man that He shall lie, nor the son of man that He should repent[47]. Job questioned, but he still went through. Jonah ran from it, but he still went to Nineveh. Jesus, even in his flesh asked for the cup to pass, but was obedient to His calling. Again, our contentment in Singleness is a journey, not a destination.

As in any other voyage, we will experience good and bad, successes and failures; the important thing is to stay on the path to where you want to be. Miley Cyrus even understood that it was about the climb, not necessarily

---

[47] Numbers 23:19

about getting to the top[48]. You are guaranteed to have pitfalls and hard times. Kirk Franklin said that every day may not be perfect, but it doesn't mean that it doesn't have purpose[49]. You will learn something out of those bad days and they will make the good days seem all the more sweet. We learn in the valleys so that we can enjoy the mountain tops.

~Christ's Love is Enough~

We discussed in Chapter 3 that an earthly desire cannot overrule an eternal perspective. We cannot be so focused on a pleasure in this life that we forget our eternal goal. Our focus has to be on serving His kingdom, everything else is an overflow[50].

1 John 2:15 admonishes us to love not the world nor the things of it. It is important to understand that this verse doesn't say, "don't desire," it says, "don't love." What's the difference? Remember the first commandment, "Love the Lord your God." God should be the forefront and pinnacle of everything we love, and all of what we desire should be filtered through that love. Desiring marriage and a mate to fulfill Christ's example of His love for the church is favorable, but loving the idea of marriage is very dangerous. If you don't agree, refer to Chapter 2 and the lesson learned from my broken engagement.

---

[48] Miley Cyrus-It's the Climb
[49] Kirk Franklin-Smile
[50] Matthew 6:33

We can't have the mindset that we missed out on some earthly pleasure if we don't get married. We were saved to share the Gospel with others through the love of Christ and then commissioned to make disciples. If we fulfill this, we have completed our mission on Earth for Christ. All the rest is just details. Sometimes this is a hard truth to accept because we are flesh, and our flesh desires instant gratification. It's a daily struggle to seek God's kingdom first (Matthew 6:33) without focusing on all those other things we want added to us. It's a practiced art, one that is only perfected through—you guessed it—practice.

~Allow God to Woo You While Single~

Someone asked me to describe what it felt like to be in love and all I could come up with were actions. My conclusion: love is not butterflies; it's the choice of a commitment that drives you to perform actions that in turn induce those butterflies in the one who has captured your affections. As a result, this causes you to feel the same "flutterings" in response.

We love God because He first loved us and He demonstrated that love through Jesus. God made the choice to perform the action of sacrificing His Son to redeem us back to Him. We feel the butterflies when we think about the measures He went through just to buy us back, knowing we would often turn away and place things before Him. The butterflies overtake us when we think about how great His love is for us, which produces joy in Him. Then as

71

stated in Psalms 149:4, the Lord will take delight in us. People love you for what they know about you, but God loves you for what He knows about you and even what you don't know about yourself. Now, that's love.

Christ's gift to us is Himself. That's it. Everything else is an added blessing. God doesn't have to bless you with this item or that thing, because John 3:16 clearly says that the gift of Christ is eternal life, not the promise of a prosperous (in worldly terms) life. Now, because of His character, He not only fulfills our daily needs but also gives us more than we deserve and nothing that we have earned. But I had to realize that He is not obligated to give anything except the exchange of His life for our sins' atonement. It took me a long time to understand this because I had always heard that God would give me all this extra stuff. So when He did bless me tangibly, it was great because it was in line with what I thought he should do, but when He didn't, I was devastated. I have now realized that it wasn't because He was acting outside of His character, but because I didn't know His character.

Christ has come that we may have an abundant life, but what do we think of when we think of abundance? Many times what comes to mind is earthly treasures— things that are tangible. Although we give Him the glory for blessing us, we still expect to get (in some cases think we deserve) the blessings. His Word says He wants us to prosper as our soul prospers[51]. As a Christian, our souls will be caught up in the Rapture to live eternally with Him, which is the

---

[51] 3 John 2

pinnacle of prospering, so what does that look like in our earthly lives? I believe it means living a life worthy of the life that was exchanged for ours. That is the abundant life—giving of ourselves through the gift that God has given us.

Take God out of the box of what your mind can imagine. We will never be able to understand His ways or thoughts. Honestly, I don't believe fully understanding God or fully grasping His magnitude should even be our goal. Our goal should instead be to continuously seek and want to know Him and He will continue to reveal Himself to us. If we could understand God's ways, why would we need faith in Him? If I could predict what He would do and how He would do it, then I would begin to think that I could just do it for myself and there would be no need for faith because I would already know the end result. Having faith in God means to trust Him to be God. He is sovereign and all His ways are just, and our faith should rest in that.

So from this reasoning, if God is enough do we even need more? Is it wrong to desire marriage or to even believe that He will grant that desire? Of course not! His love is enough, but He wants to give you more. Exceedingly, abundantly above anything that we can ever ask, think or imagine[52]—more. Christ Himself tells us to, "Seek first the Kingdom of God and its righteousness," and He will add all things to us. God created Eve to be a helpmeet for Adam, even though He could have chosen to keep Adam only for Himself. If you pay close attention

---

[52] Ephesians 3:20

to the original wording of Genesis 2:18, it reads that God said it was not good for man to be alone. God—not Adam.

God knows that He is enough for us, but He also knows that our finite minds could never truly grasp His full nature. He foreknew we would seek to relate to someone a bit more "obtainable." Although it is possible to be satisfied with God alone, He understands it is important for us as weak, flesh-wrapped beings to have someone with whom we can share this journey.

Because God loves us so much, He created a hole in our heart that only He could fill, then He created a separate one for a complement along this journey. His hole is bigger and the easiest to fill because He has already established a yearning within us for Him; we just often need help discovering its origin. He knew the risks involved—until we realize our void is for Him, we will try to fit other things into His more accessible hole; oftentimes before we even try Him. God designed us for relationships, but it's our responsibility that we not put something (or someone) in His spot within our hearts. If we do, being the gentleman that He is, He waits patiently with open arms for us to realize our mistake and place Him back on the throne of our hearts.

~He's the Measuring Stick~

If you long for emotional intimacy, I challenge you to find it in God. A man or woman may complement you, but the King of kings is enthralled by your beauty[53]. You may question if a mate loves you at all times, but you should never doubt that God has loved you with an everlasting love; that He has drawn you to Himself with loving-kindness[54].

Even in marriage vows, the epitome of an earthly commitment, the most a person can commit to another is, "Until death do us part." But I love what Paul says: "I am convinced that neither death nor life, neither angels nor demons, neither the present nor the future, nor any powers, neither height nor depth, nor anything else in all creation, will be able to separate us from the love of God that is in Christ Jesus our Lord" (Romans 8:38-39).

Everything we need as a man or woman seeking a relationship, He sets the example for how to do it in excellence. Allow Him to show you how to have healthy relationships. Use this time to begin to seek Jesus as the example of the model husband until your earthly covering comes (if it is ordained). Jesus is the measuring stick of what a husband should be, how he should act, and the example of what it means to pursue. Use Him as the standard as to the way a man should purse you as a queen, ladies; and gentlemen, seek to emulate him as a king—then refuse to settle for less.

---

[53] Psalm 45:11
[54] Jeremiah 31:3

~Christ as Father~

Christ is the example for everything we need, but He is also the example for everything that we aspire to be. Christ will show you how to have a relationship, not only with your spouse, but also with Him as Father. Man or woman, no matter how much we may try to downplay or minimize the role, we all need to feel the love of a father. This is not meant to slight the love of a mother because her love is incomparable, but I believe that the father's role in our lives may in some ways have a more direct impact on how we grow up to have other relationships.

A father is the first person that chooses you in your life. There is never a doubt of the maternity of a baby because a mother physically carries it—it can't be denied because she gave birth. But the father has the unique choice to acknowledge that the child is his, verbally and by action, before a test is given. I believe this is what gives the dynamics of the relationship with the father a different perspective. Whether you have ever thought of it this way or not, if your father is in your life, was in your life, or has ever acknowledged you without proof, then this is the first earthly example you have of a man choosing you because he wanted you, not because he couldn't deny you.

This is vital in the foundation of how you view relationships, whether you are male or female. As a female, a standard (even if you are unaware) has been set for the way you will relate with men and how they should treat you. As a male, it plants the seed of responsibility and leadership in your female relationships. Because you chose her, you love and accept her out of free will, not obligation.

This is a direct example of God's role as a Father. He chooses to acknowledge us as His children and He loved us before He saw the proof that we would come to be His. In Romans 5:8, the Word states that while we were yet sinners, Christ died for us. This is His public acknowledgement that He has chosen to be our Father, not out of obligation, but simply because He loves us. What a powerful example of relationships.

So what happens if you didn't have an earthly father to choose you? I believe it manifests in different ways in different people, but I wholeheartedly believe that it will manifest somehow. In a man, maybe it rises up when they find it a bit easier to deny their own child or how they negatively treat the women in their lives. On the other hand, they may choose to use it as an example of what not to do. He may become the protector of his mother, treating every woman the way she should be treated because he refuses to be like his father. For a woman, it may subconsciously affect her trust in men or cause her to be bitter towards men without realizing the cause. She may seek to find the acknowledgement and acceptance she never received from her father, in any man she can find to fill the void.

I was the latter. Here's my story. To preface, it was not my intention to share this in this book, and I tried to justify it by saying, "This is a book about Singles, not about fathers." I now believe it is important to share because my relationship with my father—or lack thereof—has affected every day of my Single life, up until about a year ago when God broke down that wall. Prayerfully, if sharing my story will help one person seek the healing that I didn't even know I needed, it will be worth it.

The realization of the effects of my father's rejection were probably first recognized at church one Sunday. My cousin was preaching a sermon about his daughter and his experience with meeting her prom date for the first time. He stated that he wanted to "lay hands, um excuse me, eyes" on the young man that would be taking out his baby girl. He needed to look him in the eyes and let him know he would need to climb many a mountain and swim some pretty deep seas to even get close to making the kind of impact in his daughter's life that he had. This young man needed to know, and hear firsthand that this was his daughter and that he was the leading man in her life. This is a role my cousin (her father) had earned, and not one he was willing to give up very easily. The man had to prove himself worthy enough to even apply, much less be considered for a starting position.

As I listened to him, I began to tear up. It spoke to a void that I never knew I had. I never had a man that made sure any other man who sought my affections was worthy of my attention. My father rejected me at fifteen (I will discuss this a bit in detail in a later chapter) and so because I had no consistent male to take that place, I began to allow anyone to apply. I didn't know there should be a standard. I didn't know that I shouldn't and didn't have to waste time kissing all these frogs, because one day my prince would come. How can someone learn unless there is someone willing to teach? I have a host of older cousins and uncles who could've stepped in if necessary, but I didn't know what I needed so I never asked.

The love and affection I should have gotten from my daddy, I desperately sought in men. And when they couldn't live up to that role or fulfill the hole I had, I would move on to the next one. I didn't understand why they couldn't be what I needed them to be, so once I drained them (as we talked about in Chapter 2), I would move on to my next victim, I mean relationship. The sad part about this is that I didn't realize I was doing it until about a year ago, but the amazing part is that God had already begun to heal the wound that I didn't even know was there.

The rejection I felt from my father caused me to build a wall up around my heart and when Christ first pursued me, He loved me around it. He recognized that the pain and rejection and hurt I had locked away in that vault weren't ready to be exposed or dealt with, so He allowed me to hold on to it for a bit longer. Being omniscient, He molded the rest of my heart into one that was so soft and yielding to love that I gave it to everyone I encountered. He gave me the character to love everyone deeply and wholeheartedly, to genuinely pursue relationships, to make everyone feel welcome… all the while with me tightly holding on to my hidden wall. He pursued me as lover because that's what I understood, but when He loved me, He loved me as Daddy because that's what I'd never had. And because in His infinite wisdom, He had first molded my heart to love people completely, when I was met with His love, I had no choice but to fall head over heels, madly in love with Him. This is where my healing began.

Why did it take so long for God to reveal my hidden vault? I think that I wasn't ready until then. My faith wasn't strong enough. With the recent passing of my father, God was able to reveal to me that although I had forgiven him a long time ago, I still subconsciously held on to the hope that one day my father would come back and tell me that he was sorry for the years apart, the rejection, and confess he really did want me. I was still wishing after 15 years, the one man that should have always wanted me, would want me. When that hope was buried with my father, God knew I was ready to uncover the wall. He also knew that I would be so broken and devastated by the discovery of it, that I would be ready and willing to give it to Him to heal.

He was right. And as I write this, the healing is still in progress. Not unlike a gunshot wound, God had to first take out the bullet of rejection by bringing it to my attention and allowing me to let go of the hope of reconciliation. Now He is stitching me up. On the outside the wound may look healed, but the tissue is still being repaired underneath. This is not a quick process and sometimes the smooth exterior will fool even me and I will overextend. That's when I feel the twinge of pain and realize that He is still working on me. This may be my thorn[55], so to speak (a

---

[55] 2 Corinthians 12:7

constant reminder not to fill that hole with anything but God's love and acceptance). Even now when I doubt that I can make it through and truly heal this heart, He reminds me that my weakness is the perfect place for His strength.

~Commit to Wait~

Once you have committed to becoming whole, commit to get everything out of your Singleness that God has for you and then commit to wait. When you're truly in love with your heavenly Husband, the wait for an earthly spouse is not only bearable; in many cases it's favorable. Like taking a slow stroll, you look forward to the destination, but you sure enjoy the journey. God wants to commune with you in the cool of the day[56].

When you commit to wait for your mate, know that you have now given God permission to test this vow. The Bible says we are not tempted by God, but I believe He does test our faith. God wants to know that we are choosing Him because He is first, not because there are no other options. It is easy to say we are delivered from something when we are no longer faced with the temptation of it.

I once heard Tye Tribbett say, "Deliverance is not the absence of the temptation, but the strength to resist it when it's staring you right in your face." The commitment to wait is not truly established if no one is approaching you; that's lack of opportunity not the strength of resistance. It's very

---

[56] Genesis 3:8

important to understand the difference because the enemy will test your commitment to anything you have vowed to God. Ephesians 6:13 says, "Be prepared. You're up against far more than you can handle on your own. Take all the help you can get, every weapon God has issued, so that when it's all over but the shouting you'll still be on your feet (MSG). You have not made a vow to another person but a vow to God, so know that if you truly want to uphold it, He will give you the strength to endure.

Remember as we discussed in Chapter 2, waiting is not simply twiddling your thumbs—it's active. There are things you could and should be doing in this season to prepare you for the next one. The balance is not to focus so much on the future that you don't live in the present, but also not to be so bound to the present that you fail to prepare for your future.

Commit to pray for your mate right now as you anticipate their arrival. If you desire marriage and you believe that God has given you this desire, then begin to intercede for them. This may take crazy faith to pray for someone that you may not have ever met, but if you two are to become one, you already know them.

I once read a story about a woman that kept a journal in which she wrote notes and specific prayers for her future husband. When she got married, she gave the journal to him and as he was reading it, he started crying. She began to comfort him while inquiring about the emotional response. He told her that one particular week in her journal she wrote that she was fervently praying for God's comfort and peace for him; that he was very heavy in her spirit at that time. She recalled the week and said she could hardly sleep at night because she felt such an overwhelming feeling to pray for him. He then told her that this very week was when he had lost his mother. They were both stunned and in awe. That's the kind of God we serve. He is orchestrating our lives even when we don't understand.

After remembering that story, I've now started a journal. I started it the day I found out my father passed. I really needed to express to my best friend what I was feeling and put down all the mixed emotions that were filling my head. The Spirit told me to write it down and my soul decided to write to the one whom it already loved.

I am now entering all of the good, bad, and what I believe may be unlovable aspects of myself and opening them up to him. I have decided to give it to my husband on the day before our wedding because I figure if he can read the things about me that I have told no one but my Savior, and still meet me at the altar, than he truly is my bridegroom. I'm not suggesting you do this per se, but pray and ask God for guidance in His will for you. Find your coping mechanism: the thing that will help assist you in committing to wait for your "One".

If you are not ready to commit to wait, be honest about that. We will discuss the importance of this decision in Chapter 7 and maybe that will help make the decision a bit easier.

~Loneliness Revisited~

Don't dwell on your Singleness in regards to not having someone to share things with. This will only amplify your loneliness. Although it is true that you are alone, you choose to be lonely. You can be comfortable alone; you just need to learn how as we discussed earlier. Remember that you are only alone in a physical sense, for John 16:32 says your Father is always with you. Give your loneliness to God and allow Him to rid you of all anxiety[57].

Get active and social. This is a time that you can spend with your family and friends which may become limited after you get married. Use this time to cultivate and learn how to have meaningful male and female relationships. As females, we may seek out these relationships possibly a bit more than males. Use this time to learn healthy boundaries and really build a foundation that will sustain after the wedding. Make it a point to understand that every male is not a potential mate & every female is not best friend material. You will need these real friends possibly more after the "I dos" for support and prayer.

Stop rocking your own contentment boat. I find when Single people get together, the conversation automatically gravitates to relationships and marriage. We act as if there isn't anything else to focus on in our lives, like family, friends, work, school, vision, ministry, or purpose. What happened to these? Stop talking about relationships All The Time. Although it is natural to want to talk about them, it becomes detrimental to your contentment if this is the topic

---

[57] Psalm 25:16-17

of all your conversations with your Single peers. You will begin to lose sight of all the other aspects that fill your life while you dwell on what you think you're missing. Find other topics to address and fill your mind with the many blessings that are before you right now. Discuss what God is showing you in your Single life: your last trip, your family vacation—anything besides why you are still Single and how miserable you are because of it.

One exercise that our Singles ministry did was make a list of things that they had done, or that were in their plans to do, which were easier to do within their Single season. For instance, I went on three different week- long trips, for three different reasons in three consecutive weeks. I couldn't do that (easily) married so that was a perk of being Single. Highlighting the advantages of our Single life doesn't mean that we desire marriage any less, just means we are enjoying the trip of getting there.

Remember your Bridegroom has chosen you, called you, and has given you an eternal, unbreakable commitment more solid and sure than any promise an earthly man or woman can make to you. His grace is sufficient, for His power is made perfect in your weakness. Loneliness comes when we take our eyes off the Savior and start pitying self. I'm convinced that it is impossible to have a heart full of prayer, a mouth full of praise, and still maintain a head full of worry. Need something else to think about besides relationships? Start with Philippians 4:8.

~Choose to be Successful~

If you are not content, fight to get there. Read books, go to seminars, talk to your pastor, participate in a support group—whatever you have to do to get there, do it. Don't allow the discouragement of not being there, rob you of the chance to ever obtain it. Don't sacrifice the freedom you have in Singleness by binding your mind in a cage of marriage-obsession. Free your mind and the rest will follow. Acceptance of the feelings of discontentment (and that you don't know how to become content alone) is the first step in the journey.

Get a mentor, a prayer partner, an accountability friend—whatever is necessary to help you focus on Christ in this season of Singleness. If you still find yourself struggling with the concept, find someone who may understand it a bit better and glean from them. If you desire marriage now, find a married couple willing to be real with you about the ups and downs while walking the sensitive line of not shaking your contentment. For the ultimate example of the Single life, look to Christ. Because He was consistently about His father's business, He was content in every state He faced.

God wants to change our focus. Living fully and freely for Christ as an unmarried believer will require a change of our attention from preoccupation with marriage to preoccupation with Christ. Use your gift for its intended purpose. The only way to avoid being distracted by the world and what you think you are missing is by staying focused on God. Oftentimes, we allow distractions to speak louder than we hear the Holy Spirit's voice. Whichever focus or mindset we feed the most will grow stronger, whether it is contentment or despair. Colossians 2:6-8 speaks of our roots running deep in Christ. This is the way to combat loneliness, desperation, doubt, and anxiousness while waiting; taking root in Him and allowing Him to build us up. Refuse to be easy prey for the enemy. When he comes in like a flood, allow the standard of God[58] to be set and shown as roots that run deep enough not to be shaken so frivolously.

~Enjoy the Ride~

So what does this look like? How do I become content Single knowing that I desire to be married? My answer: you have to realize Singleness is not a holding ground until you get married. Being satisfied Single means that although you patiently and expectantly anticipate marriage in the future, you actively and wholeheartedly serve God in the present. Miss this, and miss the entire purpose, power, and blessing of being Single.

Being Single but being preoccupied with marriage is like going on a cruise ship to Jamaica, but spending the entire trip looking over the rail waiting to dock. Although the cruise ship was never meant to be your final destination, the makers of the ship sought to make sure you enjoyed the journey to the fullest. If you have ever been on a cruise ship, you know most have packages which are all

---

[58] Isaiah 59:19

inclusive; once you step foot on the boat you are entitled to everything the ship has to offer. They know that your main focus is to get to Jamaica, but they want to make sure you never forget the journey. But if you stay on the deck, constantly and anxiously looking towards the horizon for even a glimpse of hope that your destination is near, you've missed all the fun of the journey. Once you do arrive, everyone who took advantage of what the boat had to offer is getting off talking about how much they enjoyed the cruise. And although you both get to enjoy the same destination, you are stuck wishing you would have taken advantage of the benefits of the ship as well.

Either you can enjoy the perks of the cruise (all the great things God has planned for you while single) or you can spend it staring at the horizon wishing "it" would get here already. The journey will take the same amount of time, but our perspective on it will be very different. Those who enjoyed the journey will say, "Whoa, I'm here already?!" Those that wasted it will say, "What took so long?!" The longer you spend fixated on the destination, the longer the journey will seem. As my mama says, "A watched pot never boils." The sooner we take our eyes off it, the sooner it will happen. God has some things He wants to show you during the journey, and if you don't focus on the here and now, He may postpone your future until you refocus on the present.

~5

Don't Let Your Vision Die

"Write the vision and make it plain on tablets,
that he may run who reads it. For the vision is yet for an
appointed time;
but at the end it will speak, and it will not lie. Though it
tarries, wait for it;
because it will surely come, it will not tarry"
~Habakkuk 2:2-3, NKJV

Your vision will become clear only when you can look
into your own heart. Who looks outside, dreams; who looks
inside, awakens
~Carl Jung

What should you be accomplishing Single but you're waiting to do? Jeremiah 29:11 says that God has a plan for us, but do we really believe this? Do we really feel like God has orchestrated a Master plan for our future? And if we do believe it, are we willing to participate in it's coming to pass?

I once heard someone say, "Don't pray for something that you aren't willing to participate in." God often uses us to answer our own and others' prayers, but we may hinder their swift solutions if we are afraid or not attuned to recognize His voice. The vision that God has given you is for you to carry out, not for you to wait for it to happen to you. In this chapter, we will discuss how to understand and work our vision by reviewing a couple of people that had a futuristic vision, but were still willing to work while they waited for it to be completed. We will then discuss what may happen if we choose not to fulfill His vision for our lives.

For the sake of this chapter, we will define vision as a given task God has planted in you. This is a particular purpose or assignment which He is entrusting you to complete for His glory and kingdom. Whether the vision is short-term or whether you will be completing it until Christ returns doesn't matter as much as your willingness to be used for His purpose.

~Understanding Your Vision~

In order to carry out your vision, you must first understand what it is. I believe that God speaks a vision over all of our lives before we are born. Just as He called Jeremiah and appointed him as a prophet, He has a particular calling that He wants you to carry out for His kingdom. Have you ever had one of those moments where God was telling you to do something, and you knew it was

God because it was absolutely impossible to do it on your own, without Him? Did you doubt and question, wondering if it was really Him? Were you concerned if He really wanted you to do that? I think at some point in our Christian walks we have all tried to bargain with God to get out of our assignment because it didn't fit into what we thought was our comfort zone. I will admit I have and if you haven't yet—keep walking with God and you probably will.

We will never understand the mind of God, but that doesn't mean we should stop trying. Our focus should always be on getting closer to Him, learning more of His character, and becoming more attuned to His voice. This is the only way that we can understand He has a plan for our lives and to ever hope to realize what it is.

The Bible states all gifts are given by God and are useful for edifying and building up the Body[59]. Notice it says useful for the Body, not for yourself. Many visions that we may participate in and are called to aren't specifically for us, but for the lives that God wants us to touch. Some things we go through God allows because He knows we are strong enough to endure them and still come out giving Him the glory. Then, the amazing God we serve gives us the divine appointment to cross paths with someone else that is going through or will go through the same things we just came out of.

Our purpose then is to use our testimony to help them overcome the very things that He brought us out of[60]. We

---

[59] Ephesians 4:11-13

are all connected in the Body of Christ and we all need each other. What I wasn't strong enough to face alone, God sent you through for me, then sent you to me to help me through it. If you are the only one that stands to gain from an endeavor or vision, I can almost guarantee that God didn't give it to you. Pray for divine knowledge of what His vision is for your Singleness, and then have the strength and faith to do it once it's revealed.

~Discovering Your Vision~

God has a particular vision for you and it will benefit others in the Body, but how do you discover it? What task in particular were you created to perform? This answer will come a lot easier for some than others. Noah was called to build the Ark, Jonah was called to go to Nineveh; these both were pretty clear cut visions with precise directions on how to carry them out.

Some of our visions will be as crystal clear as these, but many will take a bit more discernment and searching to uncover. Job was called to suffer at the hand of the enemy to prove his faith and allegiance to God. It never says that God informed Job of why this was his vision or if Job ever understood what the true purpose was behind his suffering. In fact, he was admonished for questioning the ways of God. It's human nature to question God when we are given a vision that doesn't seem to make sense, or one we don't believe we "deserve." We must understand that many of

---

[60] Revelation 12:11

our confusing or hard visions are to bring God glory and are not necessarily a direct result of some action that we did or did not do.

Sometimes our vision has nothing to do with us directly, we are just being used as the vessel that God has chosen. A prime example of this is found in Exodus 14. The Israelites were lead out of Egypt by Moses and seemed to have a clear shot to the Promised Land, but then God's Provision System (GPS) lead them to be surrounded by mountains with the sea in front of them and a bunch of very angry Egyptians behind them. The key to understanding this passage is in verse 4, "Then the Egyptians will see that I am the Lord." The Israelites' journey was a plan for God to showcase His power and glory; they were merely the instrument He used. Our vision is to give glory to God and bring others to know of His power and provision.

Because of his obedience and trust in God, Job determined to carry out his vision no matter the consequences, even when he didn't understand why it was happening. He lost everything except his life and his wife, yet he found favor in God's eyes and was blessed greater in his latter than his former. Obedience is truly better than sacrifice. James 1 advises us that if anyone lacks wisdom he should ask God who gives generously without finding fault. Discovering your vision will take work and dedication. It will take prayer and sensitivity to the voice and character of God. This is the most important aspect of discovering your vision: asking God for revelation.

~Passion, Calling, and Hobbies~ *insert lead magnet*

One strategy I used to assist me in determining my vision from God was to separate my passions, callings, and hobbies. Let's start by defining them in the way they will be used in this chapter, as to get a better understanding. A passion is something that you desire to do so much that, if given the opportunity, you would do it without pay. This is what gets you out of bed in the morning with a smile on your face, knowing you will be able to accomplish it that day. A passion takes dedication and hard work, although it often won't feel that way because you enjoy doing it that much. A calling is something that you know God is instructing you to do. It could be the thing that you are the most passionate about, but it doesn't have to be. It is the vision God has given you to carry out. A hobby is something you enjoy doing when you get the chance. This may be something you do in your spare time or a favorite activity you do to unwind. It is that thing that you would like to do, but one of the things that can be put on the back burner if you don't have the time to invest in it.

Now that you understand the difference, take time to figure out what goes into each category. Take the time to differentiate the three. For example, write out five passions. What are the five things that if you could, you would do these and only these for the rest of your life, and be fulfilled? Spiritually, we know that you would love to praise God and worship Him all day. These are a given so they don't need to be on the list. This is the time to tap into your personal preferences and natural desires then write those down. For example, your five passions could be:

1) Working with children
2) Singing and songwriting
3) Acting or performing arts
4) Being a Principal of a charter school
5) Being an at-home parent

These are *your* passions, so they can be as broad or as specific as you would like them to be.

Next, evaluate your calling. This will take prayer and time alone with God for Him to reveal His plan for your life. This may be clear-cut but will often take some real soul searching. Sometimes you will find that your calling is in line with your passion, but this is not always the case, so don't be disappointed if it's not. This doesn't mean that you can't still pursue some of your passions; it just means your calling needs to have top priority. For example, your calling may be to be the youth pastor at your church. If you refer to the example in the list above, many of your passions can be encompassed in your calling; just a bit differently then you may have envisioned. Being the youth pastor, you are working with children; you may be able to develop a creative worship arts department that includes singing and acting, as well as having a pretty flexible schedule allowing you to spend more time home with your kids. Exercise your imagination; if God has given you the passions and the calling, ask Him how to interlace the two.

Now let's discuss determining your hobbies. Many times these will be done in your down time as a way to relax. I have many friends that have actually turned their hobbies into side businesses so this could be a possibility, as long as it does not take away designated time from your calling and your passions.

Remember this is just a starting point of determining your calling from God. Rely on His Holy Spirit to lead and guide you into paths of understanding[61].

---

[61] Proverbs 4:7

*Now it's your turn – use this space to spend some time separating your passions, calling and hobbies and figuring out how the all can intersect. Remember, if these desires are from God – they *will* all fit. More about understanding the difference between the three and how the relate specifically to you is located on my website. Go to www.lavoniartryon.com for a downloadable copy and more information.

Passions:

1. _____
2. _____
3. _____
4. _____
5. _____

Callings:

_____

_____

Hobbies:

1. _____
2. _____
3. _____
4. _____
5. _____

~Working While You Wait~

How would you react if God revealed to you a vision that may not come to pass in your life span, or if He starts something with you that He has ordained to be completed by someone else? David's desire was to build a temple for the Lord's presence to dwell in, but this wasn't God's plan. He had already chosen Solomon, David's son for this vision. David could have questioned God, or tried to bargain in order to build the temple, but he didn't.

2 Samuel 7 describes how David worshipped God in awe that He would bestow great favor on his family; so much that even his offspring would be blessed. Because David's ultimate desire was to please God and not gain fame or recognition for himself, he recognized that it didn't matter whether he was the one to fulfill it or someone else—as long as God received the glory from it. This may have been a fragment of why David is remembered as a man after God's own heart. God had a different vision for David, and David accepted it wholeheartedly. Here we can see a contrast between David and Saul: David was humbled that the Lord saw fit to raise someone else up to do a work for Him while Saul burned with jealousy when he was not the one being acknowledged or praised[62].

Understand that jealousy over someone else's gift,

---

[62] 1 Samuel 18:8

vision, or talent is directly telling God that you are not pleased with the plan He has for you. You are indirectly telling Him you can make a better plan for your life by not accepting His, because you believe He is short-changing you by not giving you what He saw fit to give someone else. This is extremely detrimental to your relationship with God and it casts light on a very wrong perspective.

In Matthew 20, the mother of two of the disciples approached Jesus and asked that her sons be granted the privilege to sit at His right and left hand when He came into glory. A couple of chapters before in the same book, the disciples were arguing over the same thing: which of them would be greatest in His kingdom. Being envious of others or seeking for God to make your name great takes the glory off of Christ and puts the spotlight on you. Do a quick self-check. Ask yourself: What if the vision you wanted to carry out was fulfilled by someone else? Would you be joyous that the vision came to pass, or would you be envious that you weren't the one to do it? If your honest answer is jealousy, your motive for carrying out the vision may not be to bring glory to God or meet a need that you see in the world; it could be to bring praises to your own name. Check this perspective and do what it takes to change it quickly. Remember we serve a jealous God who won't share His glory[63].

Learn from the example of Elizabeth. When Mary came to visit her, she was overcome with joy that Mary was chosen to bear their Lord Jesus. Her husband had the same

---

[63] Exodus 20:1-5

spirit, and was humbled that his son would be chosen to prepare the way of the Lord. There was no jealousy or envy that Mary's calling was "higher" than theirs—only joy that they had been chosen to be used by God. We should live and serve by the same humility, as we will discuss in a moment.

So back to the original question: what do you do when you know that the vision you are given won't come to pass in your lifetime or maybe even in your generation? Do you sit and wait? Do you proclaim what "thus said the Lord", and then sit back to wait for its manifestation because your part is complete? I would hope not. God may use you to reveal a coming glory, but you can be assured that He still has a right-now purpose for you to partake in.

Isaiah, Moses, Micah, and Jeremiah all prophetically spoke of the coming Christ; the much anticipated Messiah. This was a major vision from God. If any vision would warrant a "one-hitter quitter", I would think that being entrusted with the task of prophesying the way of the Savior of our world would be at the top of the list. After carrying out the vision of telling the Israelites about their coming Redeemer, there couldn't be anything else that God was calling them to do, right? Wrong. God gave them a vision that they wouldn't live to see, but He still gave them a purpose while they waited for the One that He would send. They didn't sit down and just wait for the Messiah; they continued to be available for the Lord's service.

Let's take a closer look at each of these prophets' particular vision and how it was fulfilled. Each one of these prophets was given a unique calling in addition to proclaiming the coming Christ. I believe that by taking a brief glimpse into their lives, we can gain encouragement to carry out our own visions.

Isaiah was, in the opinion of many theologians, the greatest prophet of the Old Testament. Prophets, true prophets, many times weren't very well received because their call was to declare the Word of the Lord, not just good things that would make the people feel all warm inside. To a people living in sin, the Word of the Lord was not something that they wanted to hear because it shined light on their sinful lives. It called for them to confess, repent, and turn back to the Lord, and spoke of the coming judgments they would face because of their wicked ways.

Such was the case with Isaiah. He was given the task of proclaiming that a child would be born, whose kingdom would be without end; a King that would establish the throne of David forever. This is great news, right? The Israelites could rejoice because their coming Savior would "soon" be there. But this was not the case. God had already told Isaiah that many would not listen to his words because their hearts were hardened to the Word of God. The Israelites' ears were closed to God's message before Isaiah even opened his mouth, and God told him that this would be the case.

Isaiah's obedience should be noted here. He still spoke the Word of the Lord because he understood that even if everyone would not repent, there would be a remnant that would turn back to the Lord[64]. Isaiah understood something that is very hard for us to grasp today. We are not called to produce a result from what God instructs us to do; we are only called to be obedient to carrying out the vision. God supplies the increase, not us[65]; our job is to plant and water the seed. Isaiah continued to preach the Word even when it felt like no one was listening.

Do you have the same faith? Would you continue to perform the vision that you know came from God if you didn't see any fruit of your labor? Sadly, many of us would be discouraged and give up, or start to question if God had really said what we thought we heard. I encourage you to press on like Isaiah; God is raising up the remnant that your vision is touching. Remember, His Word will not return void[66]. If God gave the assignment, know that it is having an effect; it just may not be meant for you to see.

Micah's story is similar to Isaiah's in many ways. This is a book that I haven't heard many sermons on, and one that I have to admit I often overlook. I advise you to read it and soak it in. It is rich with God's character. Micah was charged to speak of God's justice to those who used ill measures to gain profit. He spoke out for those who were oppressed and often forgotten, those that didn't have the authority or know-how to speak up for themselves.

In modern days, Micah would have been considered a pro-bono lawyer of sorts. He took the vision and spoke up for those who were being mistreated by the rich and

---

[64] Isaiah 10:20-21

[65] 1 Corinthians 3:6-7

[66] Isaiah 55:11

powerful. He proclaimed judgment from the Lord on those false prophets whose "prophecies" were swayed by whoever was willing to pay the most. These individuals were usually the teachers that proclaimed God would not judge and pour wrath on the land because His loving nature would stop Him from showing His righteous anger.

Micah's calling was to cast light on the multi-faceted God we serve—a loving God Who hates sin and is full of mercy but burns for justice. This is the God Israel had forgotten and Micah was commissioned to remind them of the true nature of God. Micah warned Israel to take heed to the transgressions they were doing, and proclaimed God's fair accusation of their callous dealings with grace.

Micah's vision was for a church that had forgotten the God they claimed to serve. He was called to declare and uncover their sins before God, imploring them to repent and receive mercy, or continue and surely face God's wrath. I can only imagine the difficulties he faced daily, being given the task to speak out against those who were rich and powerful. I imagine that many of those who were being oppressed had become hopeless in their situation, believing that these leaders were untouchable. Then God sends a man to proclaim that they were not forgotten, and that God sees every injustice that they face, and will pay back the people for their evil. Would you be strong enough to accept a calling to proclaim judgment on the wayward church?

Micah was careful to speak of God's judgment in light of His mercy. It is very hard to find this balance. There are usually two extremes: for running the risk of offending someone or being seen as too judgmental, the church has come to condone or sweep under the rug many things that should be addressed and gently rebuked. In some cases, there is an air of self-righteousness and/or condemnation towards sinners and instead of using the Word to gently restore, it is used to condemn. This pushes people who need healing and recovery, further away from a loving God and closer down the road to destruction. If God has entrusted you with this vision, it cannot be taken lightly. Use Micah as a reference for proclaiming justice while still offering the message of reconciliation with God by repentance and rededication.

Jeremiah is the last prophet that we will look at who had both a Messianic Prophesy and a right-now vision. Jeremiah was ordained by God before he was born, as we all are. He had no choice in what he would be because God had already clearly and boldly orchestrated his path. Jeremiah was to preach a coming judgment, and not unlike Isaiah, the people did not listen. But the difference here is that God didn't directly tell Jeremiah that His message would fall on deaf ears. I believe that this was the reason for much of his despair, grief, and disappointment. Jeremiah wept for the people because he had the burden of seeing the destruction that was coming, but it seemed as if he couldn't convince others of it.

This can be compared to when parents say, "You will understand it in the future," or "You can't see it right now, but you're headed for a world of hurt," or even our coined phrase for this book, "If I would have known then what I know now." They can see a future that we are blind to and their goal is to keep us from facing it.

The nation of Judah was like a rebellious teen, not believing it could happen to them until the destruction was upon them. Jeremiah's role was to declare to the nations the judgment of God. Through trials, hardships, captivity, imprisonments, and ridicule, Jeremiah stayed faithful to what God called him to do. Would we be so resilient?

Many of us would run from the calling if we knew that God ordained a vision similar to any of the aforementioned prophets. Despite the freedom of living in a country that allows us to pray and worship when and how we see fit, we barely find the time to pray and seek God.

We have used our liberties, not to serve God, but to forget about Him until we need something. I pray this is not the case with this generation of Singles. I believe that each of us will rise to the unique calling and vision God has placed on our lives, committing our time to serving Him fully by bringing about His kingdom here on Earth.

These prophets did not sit down after God gave them the vision of the coming Messiah; they continued to seek Him and received a Rhema Word of what He would have them to do in their present season. If they had stopped, we wouldn't have gotten the essence of fasting and prayer from Isaiah, lead out from Egypt by Moses, nor known our purpose or the plan that God has for us by Jeremiah. We would not have been awakened to the understanding of a just, yet merciful God from Micah. I encourage you to take heart in their stories and draw from their courage to fulfill the vision for your Single life. Remember God is with you.

~You're Not Irreplaceable~

I would be unrealistic if I believed that just because I have beseeched you to go out and fulfill your vision while you are Single, that everyone is up and running now. I believe that a remnant will turn and change when they hear the Word, but I also believe that there are some that God has to have an, "I can show you better than I can tell you" philosophy with.

For those who still don't have the desire nor see the point of working while they wait for their mate, I believe I have a word for them. These are the people that believe there will never be another "them." And this is true. God fearfully and wonderfully made you, and there will never be another "you", but please don't get that confused with being irreplaceable. God has told us in His Word that the very rocks will cry out His praise, if we be silent[67]. Are you that important that God can't raise up someone else to do His will if you won't?

What I hear resounding in my head from you guys is, "What God has for me, is for me." I believe that similar to the phrase "come as you are", the initial concept was biblical, but we have now taken liberties with it, using it to justify things which were not within its original intent. Don't misunderstand—I do believe that God has a specific

---

[67] Luke 19:40

plan for your life and He has certain things which are ordained for you to do, but I also believe that God will not rest the sole plan to fulfill His vision on one fickle person. I wholeheartedly believe that if you choose not to do it, His purpose will be fulfilled by someone else. Let me explain my conclusion.

God doesn't need you or me. Now, He loves us so much that He bought us back, but yet and still He will not hesitate to dismiss one of us if we refuse to be used for His glory and purpose. Ask the Romans who were given over to their reprobated mind[68]. To illustrate, look at Moses' generation of Israelites, Ahab and his wife Jezzy, and the list could go on and on. It is an honor and a privilege to be used by Him, but as He so eloquently states in Psalm 50, the cattle on a thousand hills belong to Him and if He were hungry, He wouldn't bother telling us because there is nothing we could offer Him.

Everything that we ever give, we give back. That's a concept I believe many Christians don't understand (if we did, more would tithe). God doesn't need us but He wants us, and that makes a huge difference. Remember the example of a Father's love? God chose us without proof that we would be His. All we can offer Him can't compare to Him because everything that we have, He gave us in the first place.

I liken it to parents giving their kids money, then dropping them off at the mall to buy a Mother's Day gift. Although technically Mom bought her own gift, the fact

---

[68] Romans 1:28

that the child took what was given and used their judgment to give back something that may have had the same value, but was worth so much more is priceless. Remember the difference between value and worth. I believe that's how God views our vision and purpose. The life He gave us, He gives us the right to cultivate, grow, and use it in the way that fits our particular personality and calling, all so we can give it back to Him. What an amazing thing.

So what happens when we are like the unwise servant who chose to hide the talent instead of using it to build his Master's kingdom? I will use two very specific examples to show that God will accomplish His vision and His plan, whether you decide to participate or not. Saul was anointed as king over Israel in 1 Samuel 10 and was proclaimed a blessing over everything he touched because "God was with him" and praised because "there was no one like him."

This was a great day for Israel and I can only imagine a greater day for Saul. Samuel blessed and appointed him to be ruler; this was his vision and his purpose was to lead the Israelites. But keep reading because in just a few flicks of the wrist in Chapter 13, Saul is rebuked by Samuel for using his own judgment, instead of God's ordinance to offer a sacrifice. Because the veil had yet to be torn, priests were only ordained to offer sacrifices, unless specifically instructed by God. With this one lapse, and because God knew his heart was not submitted to Him, the kingdom was stripped from Saul and he was informed that another would complete his vision.

How is this possible? Saul was anointed as king but let his lust and disobedience mess things up. He was rejected and replaced in the same sentence[69]. And here comes David, a man after God's own heart; even though he made some huge mistakes. David was believed to be anointed as king around the age of 16, but didn't receive his appointment until he was 30. Why? I believe the reason is two-fold.

First, and most obviously, he had to mature into a man first to complete the training and upbringing necessary to rule a nation. But I think the most important reason was because Saul was still alive. Now stay with me. If God is not a man that He can lie, and His Word endures forever, then He can't say something and then take it back or change His mind. That would go against His character and make Him as fickle as us. So with this reasoning, because God can't lie, and He had already given the kingdom to Saul, although another was being raised up to take his place, Saul had to die for that next person (David) to take his place. Saul's vision had to come to pass, or he had to die for someone else to be raised up to do it.

Now, let's revisit the phrase, "What God has for me is for me." This is conceptually true, but understand that just because no one else can get it, that doesn't mean you can't miss out on it too. With Saul dead, David was now free to fulfill what was now his vision. He was wise enough not to be replaced. Even with all of his sins and shortcomings, his heart still chased God. And this mentality put him in line

---

[69] 1Samuel 13:13-14

for another vision; to be cast in the direct linage of our Savior.

Still skeptical? Let's take a look at Moses then, because he had a similar fate. Although he brought the Israelites out of Egypt towards the Promised Land, he was not allowed to enter into it because of his disobedience. Joshua 1 opens with God speaking, "Moses my servant is dead, now then, you Joshua lead these people into the Promised Land." God further clarifies Joshua's vision by saying, "I will give you all the land that I promised Moses." Moses had to die with the vision and purpose incomplete before Joshua could take his place.

Now, considering all that Moses had done for the Lord, all he gets is, "Moses my servant is dead, now then..." seems a bit harsh, huh? Don't you think he deserved a bit more? Obviously not. Now, this is not meant to say that God was not pleased with Moses and had written him out of the Will (in fact, quite the contrary—Moses did get to see the Promised Land. Mark 9:4 reads "And there appeared before them Elijah and Moses, who were talking with Jesus." Upon researching, this mountain was in the same territory of the Promised Land from Exodus.) These examples cast light on the fact that God's work is more important than anything else is! It takes precedence over everything. Remember God is not a respecter of persons[70].

God's purpose will be accomplished and if you aren't willing to do it, then there is a David or Joshua that is waiting on the bench to be put in the game. So to end with

---

[70] Acts 10:34-35

the beginning: will you give it your all while you're still in the game or give your spot up to someone who is just waiting to take your place, and walk into your Promised Land?

~6

Losing Your Potential(s)

*In [this] freedom Christ has made us free [and
completely liberated us]; stand fast then, and do not be
hampered and held ensnared and submit again to a yoke of
slavery [which you have once put off]*
~Galatians 5:1 AMP

*A wise man learns by the mistakes of others, a fool by
his own*
~Latin Proverb

At first glance, the title of this chapter may not make sense, but hopefully by the end, you will understand what it means and you will seek to live a Single life with no potentials.

What does it mean to lose your potentials? It's probably not what you are thinking. First, let's take the definition of potential and break it down so that you will know what it is that you should be losing. Webster defines potential as "possible, but as of yet not actual; expressing possibility; capacity for development." So how would this relate to a Singles book? I think by now most of you have figured it out, but for those of you who may not have put it together yet, let me expound.

For the sake of this book, a potential is a person who is hanging around, having the "potential" to be something more, but has not materialized into anything substantial at this point. If you have ever heard someone use the analogy of dating as a basketball team or car, then potentials would be your bench or spare tire. Basically, these individuals may not be needed for an extended amount of time, but you feel more comfortable with them there "just in case." Therefore, from this definition, a potential would be someone you are not in a relationship with, and quite honestly, may never make it that far, but you still keep him or her around.

This person is someone you may not even consider boo-worthy, or worse, they don't consider you to be, but you keep them around because you like the company. If we were to be completely honest with ourselves, there is usually a motive for keeping this person around, whether it is because you are waiting for the scales to magically fall off of their eyes and they realize that you are the love of their life, or because you really aren't comfortable being alone (refer back to Chapter 4). Please don't mistake this person with a mere platonic friend of the opposite sex; this is a totally different category.

This person, or if you are like the former me, these people live in the land of "in-between." They're more than a friend, but less than a committed relationship. This is the person that you call when you're in bed and you can't fall asleep, or when you need a bit of flattery or ego stroking. They are the permanent "plus one" for parties and dinners because God-forbid you show up to two consecutive events alone. Someone may think something is wrong with you or you can't get a man. Your boys may begin to think you're lame or not the "playa" that you so desperately want to portray. This relationship is not defined (mostly by mutual choice) because there is more to gain from both parties by not declaring labels. You know what you are to each other, and that's all that matters, right? Hmmm, sound familiar?

If while reading just the opening paragraphs of this chapter you have seen yourself in more than one scenario, you may be caught up in the potential cycle just as I was. In this chapter, we will discuss the danger of being on both ends of these types of relationships, and how you can recapture the freedom of your Single life. For those of you who don't see anything wrong with this cycle, maybe after reading this chapter you will understand the emotional damage that you may be causing to yourself and your potentials (and at the least, if nothing else, be more cognizant of what you are doing).

~My Struggle Your Lesson~

Remember I disclosed that I was never Single? Well, it wasn't always a boyfriend. Many times the guys never made it that far; they just got caught in the cycle until one or both of us found someone that we actually wanted to be with, or until the strings that we told each other weren't attached became too complicated.

This had become my pattern, as much of a distinguishing characteristic as my famous 5" heels or funky haircuts. I always had a man, or a potential, or someone that I had just met, or someone who was interested in me. I didn't realize that it was so recognizable until one of my sorority sisters told me in a tough-love email. She explained that from her opinion, I was never out of a relationship—I just recycled them. She stated that she could not recall a time when I was completely free of potentials. What stood out the most in that email was that she recalled me always saying the same things about each one: "He's so different. He gives me butterflies. He treats me better than anyone else I have ever dated. I've never felt this way about anyone." It made me sick to my stomach to read it.

So what did I do? I did what any spiritually immature, set-in-her-ways Christian would do. I charged her with judging me and not knowing anything about my life, so that I could justify not dealing with any of the issues she brought up in the email. She had gotten too close to uncovering the truth, and I wasn't ready to be exposed, so I hid deeper in offense and indignation. I was caught up deep, y'all.

Ever been there? If not, I hope you never have to experience that. Let this be my struggle, your lesson. If you are like many Christian Singles and only the truly strong will admit to it, this scenario may be hitting pretty close to home.

Self-check moment: How many times in the last year have you started a conversation with, "So, I met this guy," or "Man, let me tell you about this girl"? Now, think about how many of those potentials actually turned into a relationship. Worse yet, can you recall specific details that would distinguish them from the others, without prompting? Up until about two years ago, I would have cringed while evaluating this question. I don't think I still noticed the extent of how bad I was until I would go about three to four months without talking to a friend. When we would catch up, the conversation would go from work to ministry life and then the third question would be, "So, who are you talking to now?"

When I said no one, there was silence followed by, "Really? You are always talking to someone." If that were not stabbing enough, many of them would say, "Well, what happened to the guy you told me about that you met at the gas station? ...that goes to your church. ...that your friend introduced you to that works at that place?" The part I am hesitant to admit is that if they could not remember the poor guy's name or some very specific detail about him, I usually couldn't remember exactly whom they were referencing. This was so sad because from my conversation with them, I had made this guy out to be the best thing since indoor plumbing, but I couldn't even remember his name a few months later. My God. Thanks be to the Lord for deliverance.

I would hope and pray that your cycle is not nearly as bad as mine was. But if you do see yourself in these pages,

I want to offer hope to you. If God could bring me out, surely freedom is in your future if you only ask. Let's discuss the benefits of breaking the cycles by discussing the pitfalls associated with them.

If you do see yourself in section, there's help. The Not Another Singles Devotional goes into depth of the potential cycle and how to know if you are caught in it, including exclusive action steps from each chapter. **Get your free copy here!**

~Free Head Space~

I cannot speak enough about the benefits of having free headspace. Free headspace is not having the burden of constant, persistent thoughts about a particular person of the opposite sex. Now this is not to say that thinking about the opposite sex or a potential love interest is bad, but it can get out of perspective quickly.

How do you recognize if it's excessive? One way to test this is that you notice these thoughts are now interrupting daily functions. You're probably thinking, "Yeah right, that's obsessive and doesn't apply to me." But does it?

How much time do you spend daydreaming about a guy that you just met? How many times do you check your phone at work just to see if you may have missed her call—or what about the time spent virtually mapping out your next outfit for your date, or replaying your last conversation in your head? If you admit to this, you will probably admit to reading something into each pause and phrase wondering, "What did he mean by that?" May seem small but when you add this all up, it could be a significant chunk of your day.

I will admit I have often spent time re-reading text messages and emails, then sharing them with my friends so that they could say, "Awww, how sweet," and tell me how lucky I was to have found such a good guy. Even the random thought of, "I wonder what he/she is doing right now," can lead to you stopping what you are doing to check their Facebook page or Twitter stream to see when was the last time they posted or to browse their picture albums (again). I would be willing to bet (and I don't gamble) that there are only a handful of Singles reading this book, that can't even slightly identify with at least one of the above scenarios. I've found admitting it to yourself is the hardest part.

Now that we have determined what clutters up our headspace, let's talk about the advantages of freeing it. You will never understand the value of free headspace until you have it. I don't think I could ever have imagined what it would feel like having the freedom of not thinking about what he were doing or if he was thinking of me. Even worse, the nagging of, "He said he would call tonight, but it's now 9:30 and he hasn't called… OK, now it's 10:30 should I call him? …OK, I'm going to do something else and then when he calls I won't answer. Then I will wait a few minutes and if he leaves a message, I'll call back. But if he doesn't, I will wait and call him back tomorrow because he needs to know that I don't just sit around and wait on him to call." Well, news flash Sweetheart, that is exactly what you did, now you are just playing games with yourself trying to justify it. I'm only saying this because you won't admit that you do it until some else admits to it first. So there—pressure is off. You can now change because you know what needs to be changed.

Allowing a person to occupy your thoughts consistently without a commitment is like leasing out your apartment, but never collecting rent. This person has done nothing to earn or even prove they are capable of maintaining the same caliber by which you maintain your space, but you have allowed them to squat in your personal headspace like a rundown Brooklyn brownstone. When you find yourself thinking or focusing on a person that has not "paid rent," kindly write them a mental eviction notice and vow not to take the padlock off until they catch up and pay a couple months in advance. If they refuse to, then change the locks and commit to not renting it out again until you at least check the Reference of the next applicant.

In a physical apartment, it must be cleaned up after the last person before allowing the next one to move in. Commit to free your mind of all remnants from past relationships before you move someone else in. You wouldn't move into a townhome with worn down, stained carpet, dirty dishes in the sink, and a mildewed tub, would you? Yet mentally, we expect mates to come in and clean up the mess that someone else has left. Worse still, we invite ourselves into someone else's and clean theirs for them.

I hope that you caught that I used the example of an apartment instead of a house. This is significant for one reason: an apartment doesn't belong to you. If something breaks, you call maintenance and it's their responsibility to fix it. In 1 Corinthians 6, God says our bodies no longer belong to ourselves, for we were bought at a price. I would be willing to bet that your mind came with that purchase. So now you have the privilege to call the Chief Carpenter to come in and clean up the mess that you made. No maintenance man I have ever encountered has asked me to help him fix something, so you can rest easy that God doesn't need your help either. Just give it to Him and wait while He makes you new[71], then vow to keep it that way.

Now you're free. Now that you know better, commit to doing better. So what do you do with all your newfound, free headspace? Use it to think on things that will yield a return: whatever is true, whatever is noble, whatever is right, whatever is pure, whatever is lovely, whatever is admirable—if anything is excellent or praiseworthy—think about such things.

~Friend is as Friend Does~

Now that we understand the value of free headspace, let's talk about platonic friendships. I believe that the people who don't believe that it is possible to have a platonic relationship with a member of the opposite sex are those that don't know how to do it themselves. I do agree

---

[71] 2 Corinthians 5:17

that it is a delicate situation and might need to be approached a bit differently than a relationship with the same sex, but it is definitely obtainable.

When we understand this, we now become free to look at every male that we meet as a brother in Christ and every female as a sister to be honored and covered, as opposed to a potential mate. Many times when we meet people of the opposite sex, we put them into two categories: dateable or not. We do this sometimes without even realizing it. By doing this, we have just opened the door to allowing them a free ride on the potential cycle and directly into our headspace.

Speaking from the female's perspective, we will begin to imagine different scenarios and encounters with the male that have not actually occurred—but have the potential to manifest—before a hello is even exchanged. Oh, don't let the guy flirt with us or indicate that he is even slightly interested, because we will create this whole pseudo-relationship in our heads before we even exchange contact information.

Once we start this cycle in our imagination, it begins to take over. We begin to create this persona of who we believe him to be or truthfully, who we want him to be. Everything that he does from this point on will be judged from the viewpoint that we have created. The most noticeable problem occurs when he begins to not fulfill these characteristics that we have never actually seen him portray. We now have evidence for our case to say, "You aren't the man that I thought you were." You're right! That man never existed, but you won't admit it, even if you do realize that you created the image. You just move on to the next one.

So how do we change this? It may be different for everyone, but I will share what worked for me. I started to weigh everything that a 'potential' did, by my most platonic guy friend. For everything that a guy would do, I would ask myself, "Would Terrance do this?" This put things into perspective quickly. When a guy would open the door for me, I would smile and say thank you with no further thought because Terrance opens every door for me. Truth be told, my sixteen-year-old brother opens every door for me too, because I believe train up a child in the way that he should go[72].

If a guy told me that I looked really nice today, I would weigh that by how many other people (male and female) had paid me the same compliment on the same style of dress. Doing this for a week really deflated my big ego. I wasn't nearly as drop-dead appealing, intriguing, and mysterious as I had myself believing. I need to be careful to say that it didn't touch my self-esteem because that is how I think of myself. Moreover, because I know my value and understand my worth, there is nothing anyone can do to actually touch my self-esteem because it is deeply rooted in my identity in Christ. But it did give me a dose of reality and the grandeur view I had from all these 'compliments' was quickly checked.

---

[72] Proverbs 22:6

Honestly, check your own perspective on every platonic relationship and commit to maintaining the frame of reference for friendship. Hard lesson, but one we cannot afford not to learn while we are Single. This is one of those Single problems that you don't want to take into your marriage. Just because a person is friendly doesn't mean there's more to it than just that. Many things that people do have nothing to do with you, but everything to do with their character. For example, I hug everyone, so although I do consider you special, you will likely see the same affection given to the next person I encounter.

~Boundaries in Friendships~

Let's discuss the reason that we will conveniently not label a potential into the category of friend. Usually it is because one or both have an ulterior motive. As long as defining the relationship has not been discussed, we are free to put this person into whatever category that is most convenient at the moment. In this case, ignorance can be bliss because we are free to date this person, while they are only hanging out with us.

What do I mean? If there are not clear cut boundaries and defined limitations in a friendship, there is always room for misreads to happen. You may be carrying out an action because you are interested in more than a friendship and this is the way you are showing it. For example, putting together her desk or cooking him Sunday dinner could be what you do for all your friends, but in that other person's

124

head they could believe differently. We will come back to the danger of motives in just a moment.

It may seem simple or unnecessary, but setting boundaries will make sure that both parties are clear in their status. Friends don't kiss, they don't hold hands in the movies, and they don't sleep in the same bed with each other (with or without your clothes on). You may think that this is overkill, but I can tell you from experience of how my feelings have been hurt on more than one occasion by not clearly defining a friendship. I was in a relationship alone. And no matter how you word it, there is no relationship if you are the only one that acknowledges it. If a man says that he only wants to be friends, or a female says that she doesn't see you like that... THEY MEAN IT! There is usually nothing you can do to magically change their minds and make them realize what a great catch you are.

From my own experience, and from talking to some very honest guy friends, we approach this very differently. For a female, if we have verbally agreed that we are just going to be friends but our relationship turns to doing things that we don't normally do with other friends, (cuddling while watching romantic comedies in the rain, or having a picnic in the park and feeding the ducks) we are now moving towards a dating relationship, no matter what your (or even my own) mouth says. We don't have "just friends" who we are sharing of ourselves on a deep, emotional and tragically many times, physical level. Things have changed for us, and usually we will not voice it because we are afraid of hearing the reality that you are not on the same page, and then we will lose even the pseudo-relationship.

Same scenario but for a male: if the last conversation about a relationship ended with him saying that you were "just friends"; until another conversation happens and you agree to date, you are still just friends. No matter what else has transpired, that does not exemplify that it is moving towards a romantic relationship. Who's at fault in this case? I believe a bit of both, but let's come back to that.

We must realize that if we can't control our emotions for this person, we may not be able to continue the friendship. Although your mouth may say, "he's my friend," your actions are screaming that you want more. If you can't handle the friendship because you want more, guard your own heart and walk away. Make clear cut boundaries and stick to them. Tell others so that they can hold you accountable to them. Tough lesson, but do it for your spouse. Refuse to go into your marriage emotionally bonded with another person.

~Rejecting Saul to Receive David~

One of my favorite passages of scripture is 1Samuel 16. This is the story of David's anointing as King. This chapter of scripture is so full, but we will only focus on a few relevant verses to this book. The passage opens up with the Lord confronting Samuel about his continuous mourning

126

over Saul's rejection. God asks, "How long will you mourn over Saul when I have rejected him? Fill your horn with oil and go… for I have chosen another king." These two verses are so important and speak to holding on to something that God Himself has rejected. Samuel was so focused on mourning who God had said was no longer for him that he had to be persuaded to go find the one that God was bestowing favor on.

This speaks to me on so many levels, but the most obvious level would be our hold on past relationships. The thought of holding on to something even a moment longer than God's Spirit is resting on it, seems ludicrous to even write but in our lives we do it all too often. We sit and re-read letters, and hold on to old pictures and movie stubs in a shoebox that we pull out when we are feeling lonely, which is stupid because it only intensifies our loneliness.

I can imagine Samuel remembering all the "good ole times" with Saul and weeping. I have always heard that hindsight is 20/20, but I think in relationships, sometimes the rearview mirror is a bit cloudy. I know when I was afraid of being alone, (because I didn't understand the difference between it and loneliness) I would think back to old relationships and remember all the good times, while conveniently forgetting or sometimes even reworking the details of the bad times.

Samuel had to be doing the same thing here because the Bible records Samuel being the very one delivering the news to Saul that the kingdom would be ripped from his hands because of his disobedience. But yet, this is the same man weeping and wailing over his dismissal? Sounds crazy, huh? I bet if you go back in your relationship rolodex, you have had a couple of "Samuel" moments as well. Vow to break that cycle. There was a reason he was rejected—don't forget that. Do what it takes to let go of past relationships. In regards to old relationships, when God closes a door, if we allow, He will paint over it so we can't find it even when (not if) we try. Allow God to fill your horn with oil and be on your way. Your "David" is waiting for you while you're wasting valuable time on a rejected "Saul."

Realize that no one who can or will leave you is tied to your destiny. 1 John 2:19 states "they came out from us because they were not of us, if they were of us, they would have stuck it out with us." If a person is ordained to be in your future, they will be there, even if they temporarily leave. So if they decide to leave you now, just know that they will be swinging the door the other way at some point if ordained.

One test to know if a person is supposed to be in your next season is to assess what they add to your life in this one. If they are not adding to your potential or pushing you closer to your vision, they may be hindering it. God asks, "How can two walk together unless they agree[73]?" God will not hitch you with someone who is going to pull you in the opposite direction of where He is trying to take you. Not everyone can go where God is taking you, and the quicker

---

[73] Amos 3:3

you realize that and throw your dead weight overboard, the quicker you can get to your future.

Going back to the text, let's skip down to verse 8. When Samuel arrives at Jesse's house and meets what seem to be all of his choices, Samuel was all geared up to anoint the oldest son because he looked the part. He had the stature, the status, and was probably an all-out stud. Yet, what does God do? He rejects him as well. First, Samuel's judgment might have been a bit off on this particular day anyway because he was still mourning over the very person he had dismissed. But to give him credit, in this case we probably all would have picked the same son out of a line-up to be the next king. If you research Saul's anointing as king, Jesse's eldest son seemed to hold all the same attributes that Saul did when he was anointed. This can be equated to dating the same guy with a different face and expecting a different outcome; insanity in its truest form.

You have to realize that a person can have all the qualities that you may think you want, but still not be the one that God has for you. Remember that we can't know the thoughts of God, but we can be assured that we serve a 'nevertheless' God. If God tells you, he/she is not the one—even if by what you see they fit your criteria—will you still be able to reject them? We would all like to say yes, but if we are honest, how many exes do we have that we knew God didn't want us to be with in the first place? You have to decide if you want God's created best or only your imagined best. Or, does the answer depend on which comes first? If you are tired of waiting, and haven't done your homework to commit to wait, this will be a hard question to answer honestly. I can almost guarantee that your top pick will come before God's, if for no other reason but to test how much more you will trust God and wait for His provision.

Don't adjust your values to align with your actions, instead allow your values to dictate your actions. Meaning, don't choose the available 'right now' significant other who is rated at a 3, just to try and justify it by saying, "Well, maybe he/she can come up to at least a 5." Instead, wait on your 8 and then with your favor, watch them grow to a 10.

How will you know if this is your best or God's ordained best? Glad you asked. Simple. You will know because you have now become attuned to God's voice, as Samuel was. You will know when he/she's not the one, and to wait for God to bring in your "David" from the fields. Samuel, under the stirrings of God, asked if these were all the sons. With discernment, you will be able to realize not to trust what you see, but to have faith knowing that if God has rejected what is before you, then He has to have another option that hasn't been revealed to you yet. Stop mourning over what or who (Saul) God has rejected in your life, and start anticipating your David-like manifestation.

~Settle for Jacob or Wait on Edward~

Don't judge me, but I am a "Twilighter." If you have lived on Mars or been in an underground cave for the past three years, you may not know what Twilight is. The brief synopsis: this is a book/movie saga about a teenage girl Bella, who falls in love with a 109-but-only-looks-18- year-old vampire Edward, while her best friend Jacob (the werewolf) falls in love with her. Just writing that makes me question why I watch it, but stay with me. In the second book/movie of the saga, Edward leaves Bella seemly to protect her, and Jacob makes his move.

Now when Edward left, even though his intentions were pure, he had to realize that Bella could have moved on. So here comes Jacob. And Jacob is amazing. He's kind and caring and patient and understanding (and not too hard on the eyes either). He doesn't push or rush; he just lets things happen. He is there to protect her and put her back together from the pain of losing Edward. And Bella lets him. I believe it was inevitable that Bella would fall for Jacob on some level, because it's hard to have that intimate of a relationship with someone and not begin to feel the stirrings of something for them.

So like every predictable Hollywood storyline, Edward comes back and Bella has a tough decision to make. She could be happy with Jacob and Jacob would love her unconditionally, even knowing that he would never completely have her, because part of her would always yearn for Edward. But, Edward is her air. She could exist with Jacob, but would never really live apart from Edward. Bella knows what it's like to be loved so unequivocally and to give that in return. She has had her Edward and anyone else will pale in comparison to what she had with him.

This is the point of this long Siskel and Ebert review: I think we all have "Jacobs." We have someone who loves us and is willing to lay down everything and do anything to fulfill everything that we need romantically, but for some reason it's not enough. In some cases you haven't even met "Edward," but the idea or expectation of what you could have is enough to hold you back from just being content with what is available. You will always wonder if there is something greater out there. You will question, "If I had just held on a little while longer, would my 'Edward' have arrived?"

But then, the sneaking doubt creeps in (for reference, let's say the devil) and starts to fill your head with "what if's "What if Edward never comes and I miss out on at least Jacob? Am I now destined to be alone forever? Do I dare miss this one chance? What if Jacob could love me enough for the both of us? Could it possibly work if he were completely devoted to me but I was only content with him? (And lastly, but I think most detrimental) What if I choose Jacob, and because he realizes I'm his trophy and he is only my consolation prize, he goes in search of his own happily ever after? What if he gets tired of loving for both of us and decides to find someone to fully reciprocate what he feels?" Then, you are right back to where you started: alone and lonely.

You have to decide for yourself what you will do; no one can make that decision for you. For me there is no question. I will wait. "Edward" is my other whole that will make me whole. Sometimes I do worry that he won't come,

132

and my "Jacob" will wise up and go find someone to love him the way he loves me. That's a chance I will have to take because honestly, just the dream of "Edward" is more than the reality of "Jacob."

That's a scary thought that our placeholder can sometimes be enough, as long as we don't have what we really want, and he/she hasn't wised up to realize they will never be enough. Let's talk about that.

~I Don't Want You, as Long as No One Else Does~

Have you ever been there? I know I have had that friend with whom I was OK with being only a 'friend', just as long as there was no one else in the picture I had to share him with. It's easy to lose perspective of how entangled you can become emotionally with "just a friend" when there is no competition, although it becomes painfully clear when that friend gains a love interest, and it's not you.

Why is this? I believe that because we failed to set boundaries as we discussed earlier, the line was already blurred. I started dating you, but you were only hanging out with me. This happens when those talks are avoided; when you would rather ignore the signs that one or both of you are starting to feel the pull of strings, than to risk bringing it up and facing rejection or an awkward situation.

We become free to see the person as a pseudo-relationship and even fantasize about the 'relationship' being disguised as a friendship. Women rationalize, "I'm not his girlfriend, but no one else is either." Men may start

133

thinking, "This is safe; I can handle her introducing me as a friend because she doesn't have another man in her life. I'm the one she calls when she wants to go to the movies, or needs her curtains hung, or when she needs a bug killed in the house. She depends on me and depending on me is pretty close to needing me, so it's just a matter of time before she realizes that she loves me." Don't mock the situation. Many of you won't admit it, but you have been here too.

If you are in this situation, what boundaries have been placed on your heart? Are you allowing yourself to become emotionally used in this position? Are you emotionally using the other person? Many times we don't know how deeply we are tied to a person until that string is stretched by another individual. Your hold on the bond is determined by how you handle this situation: whether you decide to bow out, claiming your designated role as a friend, or if you try to hijack the situation by planting negative seeds about the new person of interest, staking your claim as more than a friend. This situation usually gets ugly pretty fast, and only in movies have I seen the emotionally attached friend win the guy over the new love interest. Not saying it can't happen, just saying it's probably a long shot. If you have been together as friends this long, and he hasn't "found" you, it may be because you're not what he's looking for.

Although you say you are just friends, what do your actions say? I have a male friend that many people think I am (or should be) dating because of the intimate connection we have. Not too long ago, we bought into the hype and started to question why we weren't together? After a few very awkward months and several brutally honest conversations, we came to the same conclusion that we had ten years ago—we are just friends. I believe this is perfectly OK in opposite sex friendships. Actually, I would deem it healthy, if not necessary, to have an occasional reality check in your friendships with the opposite sex. Many times society will make us question and doubt that we are just friends and it may be our own actions that blur the line.

Don't let others dictate the boundaries of your friendships. Platonic relationships can exist if you want them to, but you have to fight to keep those lines clear. You may have to take a step back if you realize you want more than the other person is willing or ready to give. Remember the Bible says to guard your own heart[74], not give it up to someone else and hope they protect it. We end up getting our feelings hurt because we lie, not only to others, but to ourselves saying we can handle it, but in reality we are doing anything but.

Have random "just friends" tests of your emotions, and anytime you feel that your feelings are changing, or the other person's actions are more than friendly, speak up. A friend will address it, before it grows to be the elephant in the room. Only a coward would avoid this conversation with someone you call a friend. Remember a friend loves at

---

[74] Proverbs 4:23

all times, and it's not love to know someone you only desire a friendship with is becoming more attached to you, yet you avoid it because you don't want to hurt their feelings. Understand their feelings are going to get hurt either way if their feelings have already gotten attached. It's better to gently rectify the situation now, than to do it by introducing them to your fiancé. If you are not willing to do this, you might want to reevaluate your own standard of being a friend.

~Flattery Will Get Your Feelings Hurt~

"Flattery will get you everywhere" the saying goes, but I believe it will get your feelings hurt if you are not careful. It is very flattering when someone likes you, so it's human nature to want to keep that person around, if for nothing else but to stroke the ego every now and again.

You try to convince yourself that you are just friends, that you have set those boundaries, that there is nothing there, yet you find yourself waiting on their phone calls and telling all of your other friends about your special friend.

Flattery is one of those reasons people keep holding on when you have stated that you don't want a relationship. Yet, you are still entertaining their company, knowing that they want something you can't or aren't willing to give. I believe that a man, because of their hunting nature, will only continue to pursue if there is even a slight indication they will eventually obtain their prey. Even Steve Urkel got the chance to go out with Laura Winslow in Family

Matters, and when he did, he was hooked all the more. As much as Laura stated that she didn't like him, I believe here had to be at least a smidgen of ego boosting that came along with Urkel liking her that much. Anyone willing to continue to pursue, even after you have stated your intentions and lack of interest, will definitely feed your confidence.

You have to understand that flattery always cost someone something. If you are the object of the flattery, and you weren't interested in the person before they became interested in you, ten times out of ten what you are 'suddenly' feeling is the effects of strong ego-stroking; not the sudden stirrings of a latent love connection.

So where does the hurt come in? It occurs when you allow the flattery to lead yourself on. Yep, that's said right—when you lead yourself on. A woman leads herself on when the man says he doesn't want a relationship, but she continues to try and woo him. She begins to believe she can somehow do enough, give enough, be enough, or sadly, even sex enough to make him realize that he really wants to be with her. Then she's hurt because he finds someone else and she finally realizes that she was just a placeholder.

A man leads himself on in the same way. Just because a guy can buy for a woman things she has never had, does not mean she will make him a permanent fixture in her life; it may just mean she will keep him around until either the well runs dry, or she finds something she wants more than his money. Hard lessons; take the advice and learn from someone else's pain.

Guard your heart, for out of it flows the issues of life. Don't find yourself caught up in the emotional bond of a relationship with only the commitment level of a friendship. You would do well to realize that kisses aren't commitments and words are only as good as the actions that follow them. Don't make someone a priority that only chooses you as an option.

I was interested in a guy that would tell me he was too busy and didn't have time to date with his hectic work schedule, church, side business, son and everything else on his plate. Yet, when I did talk to him, he had just come back from a trip, or was packing for another one, or going out to this restaurant or watching a game at that party. What he was too coward to tell me, and I was too googly- eyed to see, was that it wasn't that he didn't have time (he had plenty of it), he just chose not to spend it with me. When a man or woman tells you that they are too busy with school, work, or life to pursue a relationship right now, it's usually only a half truth. What they really mean is that they don't see enough potential to make you a priority.

If your "once in a lifetime" comes into your life, I doubt you will turn them down because you are in graduate school. You will have them hold the flash cards and quiz you. What am I saying? If you meet a potential that you would like to manifest into something permanent, you will do what it takes to make it happen. If the person isn't willing to do the same, that may be your cue to move on. Don't waste your life fighting for something that isn't worth winning.

We spend so much valuable time trying to convince someone that they want to be with us, when once we get them, we realize that we didn't want them anyway. I've learned the hard way that a person will make time for what they want, and if it is not you, you might want to rethink the headspace they are occupying. If a man or woman is looking over you, then they are either not for you, or it's not your time. Either way, forcing it becomes another ugly mess that the Almighty Maintenance Man has to fix at your apartment. My struggle—your lesson.

~Vision vs. Sight~

Vision is what they could be, while sight is who they really are. This can be a very tricky situation to discern, especially if you see their potential. The key is seeing not what you ascribe, but what God has planted in that particular person. A person can have a lot of potential, but that doesn't mean they will ever unlock it.

During a dating series, my pastor asked a hard question: if the person we were dating or interested in never changed, if he were the same person in 50 years that he is right now, would we regret our decision? We have to understand that sometimes we fall for the person we believe they could be, while ignoring the person that they really are at this moment. Remember potential needs a catalyst and motivation to actually manifest. A Porsche may be able to do 0-60 in five seconds, but it is nothing but driveway decoration without a designated driver. Discernment is vital here.

Please don't take this as a shot at the "coming-up" brother because it is far from that. I know, and have heard of many a woman, that has met her husband at a time when he wasn't where God said he would be yet, but still got with him because she could see where he was going. My pastor and his wife are such a couple.

This is an amazing gift to be able to see in the spirit what hasn't been actualized in the natural realm. A close friend likes to say that some things God has placed in her husband will only be unlocked when they are joined; she will be used as a catalyst for growth in him. I love hearing these stories and get goose bumps when they work out. This is a blessing, so realize that these are not the situations that I am referring to in this section.

Consider this a word of caution to those essential characteristics, drives, and ambitions which should be seen in him but are obviously missing. Even a man who has not found or come into the full realization of his dream yet, must have a vision or dream of how he will get there. Don't get caught in the trap of a brother that is not there yet and doesn't have a plan of how to get there. Worse yet, don't accept a brother who doesn't even know where "there" is. If he is following Christ, even though he may not know the future, he knows Who holds the future, and he will be moving towards a goal, instead of waiting on something to "just happen" to him.

Even the person that won the lottery and lived a carefree life from then on had the initiative to get up and at least go buy the ticket. Those who lack this drive and divine direction may be those who aren't quite ready to be finding anyone (we will discuss this concept a bit more in Chapter 8). More often than not, you will be pulled down to their level instead of raising them up to yours.

The infatuation of the person that they could be will have you elated, while the disappointment of the person that they are will leave you broken hearted. Although that fathomed person only existed in your fantasy world, the pain it causes when they fall off that pedestal is very much real. Don't allow the illusion of what could be, blind you from the reality of what really is. Don't ascribe characteristics to a person that they have never actually portrayed. Remember the danger of creating relationships in your head before there is actually one in reality.

It boils my hemoglobin when people say that Singleness is caused by having too many standards! How does that even make sense?! If you have to lower your standards to get a person, then they are probably not someone worth obtaining. I was told by a male associate that I was going to scare many men away by being so upfront about my standards. My response: "Good, I only need one, and he won't scare so easy." Challenge people to come up a bit higher to your worth (now that you understand it), instead of slumming it for the sake of having a plus one. Know that you are worth your worth, and then start acting like it.

Don't get caught in the mindset of settling because you are tired of waiting. It would be sometimes so much easier to just be with the one that wants to be with you, than to wait for the one God created you to be with. This is very tempting on those bad days we discussed. In the haze, all the flaws and reasons why you decided that you didn't want a relationship with that person get replaced by, "Well, if he would just…" or "I believe if only she could…" Don't do that to yourself; the end result is not usually very favorable. There is a reason you are not together, and unless there is new information brought to the table, your reasoning is still very valid.

Going back to an old relationship or trying to pursue a new one that didn't work in the first place is like buying a pair of jeans that were too small, putting them in your closet, and going back a month later and trying them on. Unless you have changed your eating, worked out more, or did something different to lose weight—short of divine intervention, when you go to try on the pants again they still won't fit. The definition of insanity is doing the same thing over and over, but expecting a different result. Unless something has changed with you or the other party, the relationship will probably not work the second time around as well. Commit to Wait. Remember He never said it would be easy, He just said it would be worth it.

~Keep Your Mind in the Present~

Truly being a table of one means embracing Singleness with all the freedom and fullness that it holds. It doesn't mean you want to remain here; just means that you are enjoying the time while you are here. If you go on vacation but spend all your time worried about the work you will have when you get back, you've not only wasted your money, but your time. Commit to enjoy your Singleness and be concerned with marriage as the time comes.

God knows Where you are When His time is right to present you to Who He has for you, How He sees fit, so that you can accomplish What He has destined for you. So if we believe this is true, then is it also true that if we aren't doing what we are called to do, then When the time is right, we might not be Where we should be? Someone once said God doesn't move, but we do. If we truly let Him pilot, we will never miss out because He will orchestrate and put us in the exact place that we need to be for ministry, for a job, for a car, a house, and even marriage. God knows where you're going and where to find you when He's ready because you're ready.

Living Single in a Dating World

Flee the evil desires of youth and pursue righteousness, faith, love and peace, along with those who call on the Lord out of a pure heart.
~2 Timothy 2:22 NIV

I have stepped off the relationship scene to come to terms with myself. I have spent most of my adult life being 'someone's girlfriend', and now I am happy being single
~Penelope Cruz

At a time when it seems like everyone is hooking up, you find yourself still flying solo. And even if you are OK with this, it can sometimes be a painful reminder that your time hasn't come yet. But it doesn't have to be. As we discussed, looking forward to another season (marriage) doesn't mean that you have to loathe the one you're in right now. Throughout this book we have discussed our Single status and the benefits it holds, but it was never meant to indicate that dating is wrong. In fact, I don't believe that there is anything directly wrong with casual dating.

What do I mean by casual? This should not be confused with a serial monogamous dater. As a recovering one, I think all of the, "Where are you from?", "What do your parents do?", and "Where did you go to school?" with a new person every other month, is exhausting. Who wants to know all of this information about random people?! Since I explained in an earlier chapter that I was never Single, that means I have random information in my headspace that I can't forget, about men that I don't remember. I can think of a lot of other things that I could be using that space for.

Casual dating, for the sake of this book, is the dating that doesn't necessarily lead to marriage. Either you have decided that you aren't ready for that level of commitment or the person doesn't hold the qualifications you are looking for in someone with whom you would intend to share your life. Let's talk about each of these scenarios separately.

If you are not ready for marriage, you should evaluate why you feel the need to date casually. Is it because you're lonely? Do you just enjoy the company of the opposite sex? This is not wrong, for it is healthy to have your share of both male and female relationships but remember the discussion of motives in the previous chapter. If you are considering this relationship a dating situation and not a mere friendship, then there are emotions attached somewhere. This can become sticky because now you are getting involved with someone that you don't intend to marry, or that you don't intend to marry anytime soon.

Many people do this by staying in dating relationships for three, four, five, sometimes eight years before marriage is discussed. Do you want my personal opinion of this? OK, since you asked I will tell you. I think this is only cute with high school sweethearts and possibly college freshmen. What is the purpose of two grown, stable individuals dating for six years? If you know you are not ready for marriage, why not spend the time preparing yourself for marriage, and then pursue your mate? If I am meant to be your spouse, I will be. I don't have to date you for five years while you get prepared. Now this is not to say that you need to get all your ducks in a row precisely before you get married; it's just to open your eyes to the fact that if you are going to be with a person for that extended amount of time, there might need to be something more binding than a boyfriend-girlfriend label. And if you are not ready for that, then again—why are you dating?

Second scenario is dating individuals that don't hold the characteristics that you are looking for in a spouse. This should be self-explanatory, but obviously it's not because plenty of Christian Singles still do it. I believe that this stems from not being comfortable alone, not recognizing your worth, or allowing flattery to get you emotionally tied. I couldn't imagine test driving an 18 wheeler, knowing that I have no intention of buying one. What would be the purpose? Just to have something to do? A way to pass the time? Please. Get a hobby, work on your vision, figure out your passion, do something besides wasting emotions, energy, and valuable time with someone who won't return an investment.

I have a lot of friends who have bought into these pyramid companies of selling electrical energy, coffee, or cosmetics as a side business. Many times these individuals make money or generate business by making a sales pitch to other individuals and getting them to sign up to either buy products or join the business. I used to attend these

146

meetings as "support" for my friends, knowing without a doubt that I would not be signing up to join the company. Then I began to receive more and more invitations to come to this meeting, or speak to this mentor, and just give them "30 minutes to change my life." (Side note: these individuals are persistent and usually don't take no for an answer the first, second, or third time.) Finally, I had to do a self-evaluation and realize that I was not only wasting my time by attending an event that I had no intention of joining, but I was wasting their time by allowing them to go through their entire sales pitch only for me to say, "I'm not interested at this time." This statement itself wasn't true because I would never be interested. None of these were my passion, calling, or even a potential hobby for that matter, and although some had the potential of making me a lot of money with the right amount of effort, I knew that I wouldn't dedicate the time because it didn't fall in line with my vision and purpose.

Because I took the time to discover my vision, passion, and current plan from God, (refer back to Chapter 5) I am now able to say upfront, "No thanks. I'm not interested and I would hate to waste your time by telling you that I may be interested in the future. I'm happy for you in this endeavor, but it does not enhance God's vision for my life, so I won't be getting involved." This is very liberating and I have been told by several of these friends that they appreciate my honesty. Now my free time is spent developing my vision, instead of trying to sign on to someone else's.

What am I saying in this illustration? This scenario produces the same results of dating someone that you know you would not marry. You are taking time from pursuing your Single purpose, and you are wasting head space and emotional energy that you could be saving for your spouse with someone that will not be a permanent fixture in your life. Don't allow loneliness, boredom or flattery to rob you of giving your spouse what is rightfully theirs. If you continue to buy into someone else's vision, you run the risk of prolonging meeting your mate because you are involved with another person and now you are not emotionally available to someone else. Your spouse may be waiting on you while you are busy supporting someone else's "vision" that you have no intention of purchasing.

~Emotional Purity~

Many Single books that I read, discussions I have, and seminars that I attend speak about sexual purity and this book will be no different in that aspect. Sexual purity is vital in our Single life, and I believe it is an area that many

more of us struggle with in relation to other areas. Sexual purity is essential, but I think we often overlook the value of emotional purity. I have spoken indirectly about this throughout the book via free head space, excessive casual dating, etc., but I would like to discuss it more specifically now.

Emotional purity is making sure the information that only you, your spouse, and your Lord should know, stays that way. Many times when we get into relationships, we decide that we are going to go full-disclosure. Although the intentions may mean well, this may not be such a great idea. While I definitely believe that you should be yourself in a relationship at all times, we should be careful about how much of ourselves we divulge too quickly. Remember from Chapter 1, how giving too much too soon can backfire? There are certain things about you that shouldn't be shared until that person has "paid the cost" to be privy to that information.

If this can be likened to a movie trailer, the producers understand that if they were to tell the ending of the story during a preview, there would be no real reason to watch it. Because of this, they have worked it in such a way to intrigue and interest the viewer enough to pay the cost of the tickets to see the full film.

Taking this analogy a bit deeper, have you noticed that during previews these producers often put different scenes together in a way that is different than their actual order in the movie? There may be a certain response that follows another particular line or scene, but in the actual movie those are two separate scenes. Why do they do this? I've never been a producer (although I've dated one—remember I've dated a lot) but I believe it's for the mystery factor. The full plot is only revealed to those who actually purchase the ticket. Use your imagination and relate this to your relationships. Refuse to disclose your full plot until someone is willing to purchase the ticket, in the form of a big party in your honor with a certain someone walking down an aisle in a white dress.

~Mini Pseudo-Spouses~

Do an undisclosed amount of people know that you snore or kick in the middle of the night? Who knows your biggest fear or deepest desire? With whom have you shared the rejection you felt when your father left and your mother stopped calling? As Singles, we have to be extremely careful who we are sharing the emotions that should only be our spouse's. The same way we should exercise sexual purity, we should also guard our emotions.

Let's say hypothetically, Sarah, Bob, Rachel and Mike go out to dinner. Now, Sarah and Bob are married and Rachel and Mike just recently started seeing each other—but Sarah and Mike used to date in undergrad years ago. Although they weren't 'serious' they did spend a lot of time together. As Sarah decides what to order, Mike makes a comment about how long it always takes her to order and that she will probably send it back twice because of her specifications. Then he reminds her to be careful because of her allergies to peanuts and even suggests her wine choice. As you can imagine, at this time Rachel and Bob should be a bit uncomfortable. It's not that Mike and Sarah still have a 'thing', it's simply a portion of Mike's headspace, is still occupied with Sarah's specifics, and he may not ever forget them. So who's to fault? Mike because he should be paying more attention to his own date—or Sarah because she shared all this information with someone she wasn't 'really dating'? What's the moral of this story? And no, it's not 'never go out on a double-date with an ex', although that's something to think about.

Think about it. If he is not your husband, it is probably safe to assume that he belongs to someone else. And brothers, if God hasn't bestowed His favor on her for your benefit, whose blessing are you stealing? If you decide to bond with someone that is not ordained for you, this would mean on the spiritual level, you have now created an emotional (and God-forbid a physical) bond with someone else's mate. Now think of the definition of adultery and draw your own conclusion. Just because something has not been acquired yet, does not mean that it doesn't still belong to the person acquiring it.

In the natural sense, let's take a house on which you have taken out a mortgage, or even a car that you are still paying the note. Technically, it still belongs to the bank because you have not finished doing everything you need to do to gain full ownership of it (wow, now that'll preach). But if you were to get into an accident or have a flood and your insurance didn't cover the full bill, you would still be responsible for the cost of that car or house. Why? Although you haven't fully acquired it you arc still considered the owner, for all intent and purposes. I believe that our mates are the same way.

My husband has already been anointed as my husband; he just hasn't received his appointed time yet. Remember the situation with King David. It took him roughly 15 years after being anointed to take office. He was still the anointed king; he just hadn't been cleared to take office. Likewise, for all intents and purposes, my future mate is already ordained as my husband; I just haven't done everything that I need to do in order to acquire him. I'm not too fond of thinking about someone else subletting him until I arrive, so I extend to him the same courtesy.

Now, understand my heart in this. I am not saying that you are committing adultery by dating a guy you see potential in, then realizing that he is not the one. I'm simply saying we need to look beyond seeing dinner and intentional casual dating as something just to do.

When something manifests in the natural, there is always a spiritual aspect. We would all do well to be more cognizant of it. Prayer and petitioning God to remove any emotional and/or soul ties that have been associated with a past relationship is vital to being emotionally pure for your spouse. The True Love Waits initiative founded by Lifeway Christian Resources in 1993 focuses on sexual purity, but I also believe that it can relate to the emotional exclusivity as well. Commit to wait so your spouse can hold such a intimate place in your heart and mind that there is no one with whom they have to compare…or compete.

~Single Until Married~

The Bible recognizes Single and Married. That's it. Now, there is a betrothal period, but this is considered in the same category as marriage, which is evidenced in Matthew 1:18-19. Verse 18 states that Joseph was pledged to marry Mary, then verse 19 refers to Joseph as her husband and that to "put her away from him"—he planned to divorce her. Why is this important? I believe it places a greater emphasis on the importance of our relationship status, inclining us to take it more seriously.

If we would have to get a divorce in order to break an engagement in today's society, more of us would cautiously weigh this decision instead of speaking of marrying in such a careless way. I believe if I would have really considered the true reason behind an engagement the way God intended, I would have said 'no' to the proposal, rather than breaking it off three months before the wedding. The purpose of the betrothal period was for the man and woman to set their affairs in order to prepare for the actual marriage, as well as a designated time to become more emotionally intimate. Betrothal was a covenant and was not meant to be broken. How tragic it is that we have 'adapted' the concept of relationships to fit our society, instead of adapting our behaviors to fit the standard.

A man once told me that he couldn't join the Singles ministry because he had a girlfriend. I laughed and told him, "God doesn't recognize boo status, Boo, you're Single until married." I've come to realize many people have this same view—that all Singles in the Singles Ministry can't be involved in a relationship, which would exempt them, and they can't join because they aren't "Single." I've never read anywhere, besides on Facebook that a status change causes this much attention.

Being in a relationship is significant, but don't get misled into making it into something that it is not. Your status changes when your name does or when you have decided to share your life with someone else—not because you bought matching shirts and took pictures together. If I sound cynical here, it's because my eyes have been opened to see how cavalier we are with our emotions and how careless we are with our own pearls (Matthew 7:6). What happened to the standards of dating and the sacredness of joining lives together? Again, once we learn how to be alone, maybe then we will stop jumping into relationships so frivolously in order to avoid the 'sting' of Singleness.

Be careful not to ascribe characteristics, duties, or responsibilities of a spouse on a boyfriend or girlfriend. There are roles that only a person whom you have a covenant with should be fulfilling, and if you exert that kind of pressure on a relationship that does not have the foundation for this level of commitment, it will eventually cause huge problems or a nasty breakup.

Guard your heart, for out of it flows the issues of life[75]. Refer back to Chapter 5 if needed. Don't find yourself caught in the roles of a wife and your name hasn't changed. There is a distinct line to walk here. There is definitely reason to exemplify certain qualities and characteristics of a

---

[75] Proverbs 4:23

potential wife or husband in a serious relationship, but don't get caught up in playing a role until you have been cast for the part.

~Role of a Father~

I discussed that I didn't have a permanent father figure in my life. This has had both a negative and a positive impact on my life. Because my father wasn't there, I didn't really know how to relate to a man, and I knew nothing about submission to one. This paved the way for me to try desperately to fill this role with a boyfriend, (many were older in my younger years), because I knew I had a need, I just didn't recognize what it was. Now, God is showing me the advantage or blessing if you will, of not having this relationship.

Up until recently, I would tell people that I never had a father in my life. But that's a lie. I did have a father until about the age of 15. He wasn't much in the way that I now know what fatherhood is, but he was mine. Because I was his only daughter, I thought that made me special, and for a while I believed without a doubt that I was. So the devastation was all the more real when the one man that was supposed to love and cherish and protect me, the only man that couldn't have a hidden agenda in loving me because his own blood ran through my veins, told me he didn't want me anymore.

Remember the wall that I told you about earlier? Well, this was the first brick that laid its foundation. This pain was too much for a teenager to bear, so I suppressed it. Being a certified counselor as an occupation, I now know that the human brain can bury hurt, pain, and even entire events in an attempt to protect itself. So that's what I did. I began to believe the lie I told myself for so long: I never had a father. His death forced me to face the truth. This realization allows me to feel empathy for the women who believe having a piece of a man, or even sharing one, is better than not having one at all. If you would have asked me in those crucial years of discovering who I was, would I have preferred my daddy to have been there even half-heartedly, I wouldn't have hesitated to tell you 'yes'.

This mindset brings me to explaining the positive of this story. Because we serve a nevertheless God, there is no way that He would allow me to go through this much pain, doubt, and rejection without having a great testimony on how He was to use it for His glory. A.W. Tozer states, "Before God can use a man greatly, He must first wound him deeply." I can't explain the theological argument behind this statement, but I can tell you the truth it holds in my life. I was wounded deeply; literally a piece of something died inside of me. I now believe that in order for something to live, something must die in its place. A seed must die to bear fruit. Christ had to die so that we could have an abundant life.

My idea of what a father was supposed to be, based on my image of my natural one had to die before the true example of a father found in Abba could live in me. I don't think I would have trusted God and needed Him with the abandonment I experienced, had my father stayed in my life. God's image would have been distorted by what I saw in my earthly example. But because I suppressed those memories of what my father was, God had a clean slate to work with. He became the ideal Father without having to reconstruct an image I had already formed. Once He was solidly on the throne of my fickle heart, and firmly planted within my brain as Father, He knew I was ready to shatter the fantasy I had made myself believe to get true healing from it.

So why did He choose to reveal it to me now? If I was already surrendered to Him, effectively working in His kingdom, why not allow me to remain in my ignorant bliss and spare me the hurt? I believe it was because He needed me whole. He knew that there was no way He could use me in the way He ordained, or move me to my next level of glory, without being whole. And He also knew that the enemy of my soul allowed me to hold on to that hurt and pain, letting it slowly ebb out into every relationship I had until it was poisoned by it.

God couldn't allow that to happen again because the plan He has for me as a Single and together with my husband is too great for His kingdom to even give the enemy the smallest foothold. God had to bring the pain to the surface so it could heal, at its proper time. I truly believe now, if I never did before, that ΛLL things work together for the good of those that love the Lord and are called according to His purpose[76]. My life has been this scripture personified. They weren't all good, but He still is.

Now I'm well on my way to full healing and wholeness, and I lived through it to encourage someone else that they can get there too. God is not a respecter of persons (Ephesians 6:9); if He can restore me, surely there is healing for you.

I read an article where a man stated he wouldn't marry a woman who didn't have a father due to her not having a frame of reference of how to treat a man. I see his perspective, but challenge it to say that if she did not have a natural father, she could very well learn this role from a spiritual one. The church in many cases will act as a spiritual covering, and a woman can also pray that God leads her to a godly, natural example from whom to glean accepting that role of a covering until her husband comes.

~Let's Talk About Sex, Baby~

No matter how you word it or say it, outside of marriage, SEX IS SEX IS SEX IS FORNICATION. This is the all out, keeping it real, calling it what it is section. So if you do not intend to be real about sexual purity, you might want to skip this one right here.

What makes sex better is the emotional bond behind it. So no, you Beautiful Queen reading this who has forgotten her value, your sex is not like "whoa." And I'm sorry, Man of Valor that has never been told that your true genius is between your ears and not your legs, you are probably not the best she has ever had. Sex is meant as a blessing from

---

[76] Romans 8:28

God to be used within the sanctity and safety of marriage; anything else is sin. You cannot make "love" to someone you are not in covenant with.

If sex before marriage is sin, and God is love, then you can't make something that symbolizes a holy God while sinning at the same time (now that'll preach)! It's sex, at its best just good sex. There is no, "She is just so fine," nor is there an, "I really love him," clause… or if you are peeking into my past there is not a, "Well, we are going to get married anyway," one either. Sex is not something that you can dabble in first because you think you will get around to marriage eventually. There is no stealing home in this game. It has to be used within the intentions of that which it was meant.

1 Corinthians 6:16-20 explains that we were bought with a price; that our body no longer belongs to ourselves, but to the One Who paid for us. We should see our body as being given on "loan"—not something we can afford to replace when the Owner comes back to claim it. The Message version of the Bible really states this in layman's terms:

"There's more to sex than mere skin on skin. Sex is as much spiritual mystery as physical fact. As written in Scripture, 'The two become one.' Since we want to become spiritually one with the Master, we must not pursue the kind of sex that avoids commitment and intimacy, leaving us more lonely than ever—the kind of sex that can never 'become one.'

There is a sense in which sexual sins are different from all others. In sexual sin we violate the sacredness of our own bodies, these bodies that were made for God-given and God-modeled love, for 'becoming one' with another. Or didn't you realize that your body is a sacred place, the place of the Holy Spirit? Don't you see that you can't live however you please, squandering what God paid such a high price for? The physical part of you is not some piece of property belonging to the spiritual part of you. God owns the whole works. So let people see God in and through your body." MSG

Sex was meant to cleave, to connect and join two people as if never to be separated again. So you should expect to feel the residual hold with someone you were sexually intimate with, even after a relationship is over. Only God can break those soul ties. Go to Him and have Him restore you, so you don't take more than yourself into your marriage bed.

No matter what you have been told, Brother, you are strong enough to wait and Sister, you are worth the wait. If someone tries to convince you that you're not, tell them they are less than worthy of what you have to offer. If you have to convince someone of your value, then they are not worthy of it. It might even be safe to say that you don't know it yourself if convincing someone of it is a strategy of yours. Strength is in waiting, not giving in.

~Repentance Does Not Negate Consequences~

We have to understand as the Bible states, there is more that occurs during physical intercourse then merely an instant gratification or the release of dopamine. In the spiritual realm, you have cleaved (become one) with another individual and then when you get up and go back to your respective homes and carry on with your daily lives, this doesn't line up with the purpose that was intended for this act. Therefore, we would be ignorant to assume that there would not be a consequence for this sin.

Romans states that the wages of sin is death. Spiritually repenting by confession will cancel the spiritual consequence of sin, but it may not affect the natural consequence which is attached to that particular sin. Sexual intercourse was intended within the confines of a marriage to protect us from things such as disease, unplanned pregnancies, and emotional soul-ties. When we use it out of this intended purpose, we are now vulnerable to all of these and more. King David exemplifies this concept when he sinned with Bathsheba. God forgave him spiritually and he did not receive the wage of spiritual death, but the natural consequences were not avoided and it cost him the life of his son.

I believe that sexual sin is one of the strongest (if not the strongest) hold that Christian Singles face. There are many theories as to why this is and I believe that part of it deals with sex being seen as a hidden sin. The only people who naturally will truly know you are committing this sin are those with whom you commit it, and they have just as much to lose as you do so it remains hidden. It only becomes visible when a consequence becomes evident (i.e. disease, soul tie, and/or unplanned pregnancy). In our finite minds, we seem to worry more about our appearances to the natural man, than our spiritual walk with God at times. Remember God sees all, even when the lights are off and the doors are locked. Natural man has neither a heaven to give you or a hell to send you to; your concern should be in sinning against your Savior, not being outted by your natural counterparts.

I remember being baffled with how many Christian Singles could be serving in ministry, seemingly on fire for the Gospel, but still be engaging in willing and habitual sexual sin. I couldn't understand how a person could not feel any conviction, how they did not realize they were grieving the Holy Spirit and defiling God's temple. That is, until I became one.

In my mind, I justified it by stating I only did it in committed relationships (unaware that the only true committed relationship is the marriage covenant; everything else is simply taking someone at their word). I was still serving in ministry and believed that no one could tell, so because I was seemingly getting away with it, I continued to do it. What I was too immature to see was that it was evident in the spiritual realm. My ministry suffered, I had no power; I would pray and no one would get delivered or set free, including myself. My spiritual life had become nothing but a clanging cymbal, a resounding noise that was nothing but a mere shell of what it used to be. Yet, I had become so blinded to the spiritual consequences, I told myself that there was nothing wrong, therefore I didn't seek help. I didn't know I needed it. Only when a spiritual mother spoke to my situation directly from the Word of God, was I able to see the effects that my hidden sin had on my exposed life.

I believe that this is a key attack of the enemy, and it's one that he won't likely be changing anytime soon because it's still working. His M.O. is consistent because our weaknesses are consistent. Returning to David… he had gotten so caught up in his sin and deceit, he didn't even readily recognize his sin when it was blatantly pointed out[77]. He had gotten away with it for enough time that he started to believe the lie he had created. When he was exposed[78] he then wrote one of the most heartfelt and relevant Psalm, pouring out his repentance and sorrow. It takes God holding the mirror up to our lives and showing us that what we think is hidden from man, He always sees. It takes strength and humility to allow Him to change us, but it can be done. A lesson to be learned from David is that he accepted the natural consequences for his sin without complaint[79], because he understood that spiritual forgiveness was his biggest need.

Premarital sex separates us spiritually from God and we force our Savior to participate each time we engage in it, because He dwells within our temple. We can't simply, as

---

[77] 2 Samuel 12:1-6

[78] 2 Samuel 12:7-13

[79] 2 Samuel 12:20-23

the old folks say, "Put Jesus on the shelf for a minute." Therefore with the body that He has entrusted us, we have joined with another temple and in exchange for a few moments of instant gratification, we have succeeded in defiling us both. The next time that you feel the urge to fall into this temptation, remind yourself that your body doesn't belong to yourself and that it is a gift to be used for God's glory. You are lending out borrowed property, and at any time that you don't treat it the way it was intended, the Landlord can, and sometimes will, decide to seize the property-whether spiritually or naturally.

I feel the need to speak on unplanned pregnancy. By mostly my selfishness, and largely due to God's grace and mercy, I have not given birth to a child as a consequence of sexual immorality, but my heart is humbled by the strength of those who have. Rest assured that upon repentance, your spiritual consequence was covered by the blood, and God chose you to carry out this particular natural consequence in the form of blessing you with the responsibility of birthing a child created in His image. Your sin doesn't disqualify you from being trusted to raise a child and the situation behind your child's conception does not disqualify the blessing of their life. Never forget that. The act of premarital sex was the sin, but the child is a blessing. The latter is to be focused on; the child should not be considered a consequence of your sin, but seen as a beacon from God as if to say, "I haven't given up on you."

You could have chosen to keep your sin 'hidden' by

escaping with an abortion, yet you decided to recognize that God doesn't view us as man does, and gave your child a chance to grow into what God intended for him or her to be, before the foundation of the Earth. That is commendable, because statistics inform us that 1 of 3 women didn't have the same strength. This is not a case for being a single parent, but a mere acknowledgement that God still has a plan for both you and the child.

~How Pure Can You Stay~

Many times we play with the line and see how close we can get, instead of how pure we can stay. We want to see how close we can get to crossing the line, without actually being "in sin", from our limited natural perspectives. This is evident in conversations and mindsets when a question of, "Is oral sex considered sin?" "How close can we get?" "If there is no penetration, technically we haven't sinned, right?"

How corrupt and vile and *simple* are our thoughts. The Bible says to stay away from all types of immorality, not just intercourse[80]. God says to "Be holy as I am holy[81]". Next time you feel tempted to play with this line, remind yourself of the nails in Jesus' hands, the beating He suffered, and the shame of the cross before you decide to fulfill a temporary pleasure. I know it sobers me up real quick.

---

[80] Ephesians 5:3
[81] 1 Peter 1:15-16

I was having a conversation with a male associate recently and he stated that he couldn't understand why I was still Single and that he was going to have to hook me up with someone. Then he pauses and almost sympathetically says, "You don't have sex and you are the marrying type that doesn't just date to date, so I dunno." I responded with a smile and a thank you. What the world calls a fault, God counts as his favor. Although I can't give my husband my natural virginity, I can give him my vow of celibacy. Once I knew better, I decided to do better.

Don't be silly enough to fall for or try to use the lame lines of, "Let's just lay here with our clothes on," or "I just want to hold you." Come on now! You are smarter than that! Even my six year old niece can't sleep in the bed with me without wanting to cuddle and be directly under me. A guy once told me that we could sleep in the same bed together and not touch each other. My response was, "Why would I do that?! What's the purpose? If we are not having sex or even touching, then you can stay in your own bed and I can stretch spread eagle across my own. And since we just discussed that sex is not an option until I have a big party in my honor, its best you stay at your own residence and we just fall asleep on the phone." It's the next best thing, and I won't need to repent in the morning to repair the damage to my relationship with my Husband I willingly caused.

If we are truly real with ourselves, sex never "just happens." There was at least a thought in your mind when you invited him over that the possibility was there; ladies, that's why you wore your good panties and gentlemen, your restroom is never that clean.

Denying that we desire sex, or thinking of ourselves as stronger than we are, puts a smile on the devil's face. Doing this turns off God's power and tells Him we are strong enough to handle this temptation on our own—and we are not. The enemy of our soul is waiting to show us just how weak our flesh really is.

It's a human instinct to want to accompany emotional feelings with physical contact. There is nothing wrong with that, and you don't want God to take this desire away because you will need it once the "I dos" are said and the guests have all gone home. You just need God to still it. Even still waters have a presence and serve a purpose; they let you know that they are present, but are at peace until something comes to disrupt. Don't skip a rock in your own pond and don't be the cause of rushing waters in someone else's. God created sexual intimacy to be a lasting bond which is why Paul uses virgin and unmarried as synonymous. If you have fallen, use your Singleness as time of breaking those soul-ties and regaining spiritual purity.

~8
OK, I'm Ready Now , I Think, ummm Maybe?

Trust in the Lord with all your heart and lean not on your own understanding, in all your ways acknowledge him, and he will make your paths straight.
~Proverbs 3:5-6 NIV

If we are facing in the right direction, all we have to do is keep walking.
~Zen Proverb

Now that we have discussed being content Single and having the right perspective of this time in our lives, let's briefly discuss dating. This topic will only be skimmed because this book is not intended to be a dating manual. However, I would be remiss not to mention what God has shown me in this area.

How do you know if you are ready to date? I don't know if there is a specific formula for this. Of course, the first and most important answer is an immeasurable amount of prayer. If you are attuned to His voice and understand His purpose for your life, you will be better equipped to discern when He is ready to move you towards your next calling in relationships. Many of the things we have discussed in the previous chapters can and will apply directly to knowing whether you are ready to date with the intention of marriage. I would like to clarify that I am talking about intentional dating, to seek the answer to the question if this person is your helpmeet or earthly covering. I will not speak much on casual dating here since it's already been covered.

Refer back to Chapter 3 and the discussion of understanding your quirks and knowing yourself. Having this knowledge available will be instrumental in knowing if you are ready. If you have realized you are selfish or self-absorbed or stingy or stuck in your own ways or inconsiderate, then you should be advised that these characteristics will not mix well with marriage. Remember that you will now be considered one with another person; there is no more I, but we. This should not be taken as to lose your identity in your marriage, but merely to understand you will no longer be making decisions only based on yourself.

The only person who can tell you if you are truly ready for the next step in your life is God, and you will only hear this through communion with Him. Prayer may sound cliché, but it doesn't make it any less true. Remember, divine guidance only comes to prepared hearts.

~Casual, Committed/Group, Individual~

A dating relationship may not be exclusive until you have stated it. Don't ever assume that you are the only one who this person is seeing because the definition and terms of dating or hanging out or talking mean so many different things to just as many different people. It is crucial to define what it means to you and your prospective mate.

I believe that developed friendships here would minimize miscommunications and assumptions. If you get to know a person as a friend first with no ulterior motives, then you are free from the emotional expectations of a relationship, allowing you to get to know the real person. The pressure is off and you are free to be your real self, leaving your representative stored away until your next job interview. It's important to see a person as a friend first, not deciding to be a friend just because you know this is the 'proper' first step in relationships. Remember we discussed created personas in Chapter 6. This could apply in this scenario just as easy. If you meet a person and initially intend to get to know the person only for the sake of pursuing a relationship, then your motives may be warped and you may miss critical red flags you would have noticed in a platonic friendship state. Once we have a certain persona or image of a person in our head, we will begin to weigh all of their actions by this measuring stick.

If you meet a young lady and you believe she is interested in you, everything she does from this point on is weighed from that perspective. If she hugs you, you perceive she held you for a second longer; if she dresses nice, it's because she knew you were going to be there and wanted you to notice; if she invites you to a group event, it's because she really wants to get to know you better. Because of your perception, you have now given her an ulterior motive for everything that she does, and the real person is only seen through your rose-colored glasses. This is not fair to that person, nor is it to you.

One way to combat this is by weighing it with the "other friend" test, which we discussed earlier in chapter 6. Think of another lady friend you have that only holds the title of friend. Would she do some of the same things that the woman you're interested in is doing? If the answer is yes, trust that feeling until there is clear and concise dialogue that there is something else arising.

This being done will allow you to make clear, level-headed decisions about the person and decide whether to pursue a relationship or not. Then at the appointed time, if you do decide to pursue more than a friendship, you know the real person and you also have the added layer of commitment and emotional care from the foundation of the friendship formed.

I believe the reason many couples don't "fight fair" in arguments or disagreements is because they were never true friends before they agreed to the committed relationship. If you develop a friendship with a person, there are certain things that you wouldn't even consider doing or saying because you wouldn't hurt your friend that way. If you have based your relationship only on those butterfly feelings, when you no longer feel them, the gloves may come off a bit more freely, even landing a few hits below the belt as well—because anything goes.

Dating in groups or individually is a preference. I would suggest you at least have some group outings because the person you see alone can be a totally different person in a crowd. I dated a guy (where have you heard that before?) that treated me like a queen when we went out alone; on the phone he was so nice, sending text messages during the day with encouragement and words of affirmation about how much I meant to him… but things were different when we would be in a mixed crowd of friends.

I couldn't quite put my finger on it for a while and this puzzled me. I knew that I didn't feel the same way in both settings and I knew that he was the cause of it—I just couldn't figure out how. Then it dawned on me. When we were alone I was his priority, but when we were in a group setting, I felt like nothing more than an option. It was almost as if I was an afterthought and the connection that we built intimately was null and void. For him, I was good enough to date privately, but not good enough to claim publically. My struggle, your lesson. Remember; don't make anyone a priority if they won't return the favor, either alone or in a group.

~Boundaries in Dating~

173

I am a strong believer in the statement that if you fail to plan, you are planning to fail. This applies to relationships and boundaries. If you do not become intentional in setting and keeping boundaries, it may just be a matter of time until you find yourself in one of those "it just happened" situations. As Christians, we are to refrain from even the mere appearances of evil[82].

Back in my lust-filled days, I once had a neighbor ask me about my husband. When I told her I wasn't married, she quickly apologized with embarrassment, stating that she assumed the man she always saw coming and going from my house was my husband. Because I was so caught up in my sin, I didn't even realize that she was delivering a message from God—a warning to repent, and a natural manifestation of the ineffectiveness of my testimony.

Now that I have committed all my ways to the Lord, I have set some pretty strict boundaries in relationships. It's not because I am so holy, but rather because I'm so sinful. My flesh wants any reason to act up. A warm body lying on the couch watching The Notebook at 2 AM is like triple chocolate cake with no calories; pure delight for a sinful rendezvous. I put no confidence in my flesh, so I make it very difficult for me to fall even when I want to.

I suggest you honestly and transparently evaluate your own weaknesses and create boundaries to combat them. Once these boundaries are set, tell someone. Notice I didn't

---

[82] 1 Thessalonians 5:22

say everyone, but you should have a person who loves you enough to be honest with you at all times.

Some people, if they do not share the same convictions, will think that your boundaries are 'doing too much' and many won't understand the reason for them. For example, when I told one of my female associates that many of my male friends didn't even know where I live, and that it would be several months before I allowed a male relationship interest to pick me up from my home, she thought this was ridiculous. You have to realize that everyone won't understand what God has called you to. If that were the case, Noah wouldn't have built that Ark and the walls of Jericho would still be standing. Trust what God says and let all the nay-sayers fall where they may.

Another factor to realize when considering dating is that just because you have two Christian Singles, doesn't mean that they are yoked to be together. This is pretty obvious in some cases, but in others it may be a harder lesson to learn. You can be unequally balanced even as two believers[83]. I had to learn my mate will have to have some crazy faith because God has called me to a crazy, uninhibited faith. If God has called me to quit my job and move to Africa (please Lord don't get any ideas), then I need a mate that will say, "OK, I already booked the flights."

Your vision and purpose in life will be hindered if you are hitched to someone who is not pulling in the same direction. If I don't trust God in the same capacity you do,

---

[83] Amos 3:3

then I may be tempted to tell you (and believe it because He has never spoken to me in such a way) that "God

wouldn't tell you to quit your job without having another one in line," or something similar, if I have not heard it for myself.

I have a friend that likes to say, "Don't share your vision with someone whose faith isn't big enough to understand or believe it." Such a powerful truth packed into such a small statement. If you don't understand God the way I do or worse, if you don't have the desire to, then you will hinder me. My calling is more important than the lure of your bulging biceps and pearly whites. Again it goes to say, get to know a person first, before you invest in them. I was told by a guy who was interested in pursuing me, "You don't accept me for who I am." My response: "Yes I do—it is just less than what I'm willing to accept from my man."

~Dating Scene~

Pastor Terrance Johnson of Higher Dimension Church in Houston, Texas did a sermon series on dating a few years ago that highlighted many things that we don't often think about. Again this book is not about dating, but because it does hold a significant place in our Singles journey it will be broadly addressed. He discussed a list of questions we should ask a mate and ask ourselves before we are committed. Some of these questions I have mentioned before, but I can't stress enough the importance of knowing this person before you decide they are worthy of bestowing your favor on (or in the males case, worthy of your covering).

What's your bait? What's your sales pitch? As we discussed in the example of shopping for a car, if the only things you lead with are what you aren't going to do and what the other person has to do, you might have a longer journey than you imagine. If there are truly plenty of fish in the sea, it's important to understand that you will only catch what is attracted to your bait. That's worth repeating. You will only catch the type of fish attracted to the bait you're using. If you don't want a chick after your money, stop throwing it around and talking about what you can give her on a first date. And ladies, if you don't want a dude to want only what you can give him physically, stop showing him and everyone else the package.

A guy friend once told me, in my provocatively dressing days, that I was falsely advertising. He stated I was like a window display that was meant to draw a person into the store, but when they came in, they realized what they saw and what initially attracted them, wasn't even for sale. What does this mean? Stop showing off your boobies and your booty and then screaming you aren't having sex. You're giving mixed signals. It's hard for a man to believe that you aren't giving up what you are so ready to show. Realize your beauty comes from within. Truly live by, "What you see is what you get." Nothing.

Another issue I have noticed is how men and women never communicate the same. You will do well to understand and respect this in every relationship you hold, be it platonic or romantic. When communicating, make it your focus to not just hear, but really listen. Realize that understanding another's point of view doesn't equate to agreeing, it just means seeing their perspective. Women, please stop saying, "It's OK," when you know it's really not. A man is not a mind reader, no matter how in sync you believe you two are. It is unfair and immature to expect a man to guess what you need. Stop sending mixed signals and say what you mean. Men, know that if we still say "It's OK"-it is probably anything but OK. It would good for you to pick up on non-verbal cues and body language to make sure that what you are hearing and seeing actually line up. Doesn't make it right, but if you want peace you may have to bite the bullet on this one.

~Sister to Sister~

In order to be found, you must first be hidden. There is a popular saying that a woman should be so hidden in Christ, that a man must seek Him to find her. Make this your personal goal; to be found sitting at your first Husband's feet until your earthly covering finds you, and every day thereafter. Helen Rowland says, "The woman who appeals to a man's vanity may stimulate him, the woman who appeals to his heart may attract him, but it is the woman who appeals to his imagination that gets him." Don't be Cancun (Chapter 2); some mystery is important.

You are not the display; you are the diamond that is kept in the back and only brought out when someone walks in that can actually afford you. You may be afraid to be kept in the back room because you think that you will get passed up. Remember that the Store Owner has not forgotten about you because He placed you there. He will be able to recognize the man who is worthy because He will draw him into the store when it's time. I've heard that for every good woman there is a man who doesn't even see her. That's OK. Realize a man doesn't need help finding you. You don't have to stand out to get noticed and you don't need every man to notice you, just yours.

So ladies, how do we do this play for attention? If we are honest, we have all laughed a bit more, talked a bit louder, walked past him twice to make sure he saw us; the list could go on and on cataloguing the things we do when in the vicinity of a man who has caught our fancy, before it is obvious as to whether we have caught his. The person who is made for you will not miss you when his eyes have been opened to you, and if he is missing you it's because it's not your time. Again, in order to be found you have to first be hidden. Many of us say we want to be found, but we are not doing a good job of hiding in Christ. Instead, we are leaving maps, clues, GPS directions, and breadcrumbs on where exactly the man should look to find us. We might as well do the hunting if we are not going to be the target, which brings me to the next point.

I have recently heard this term "thirsty" to describe a female (and a male at times), but I didn't understand what it meant. I think the best description is a form of desperation, and the only mental image that I can equate it to is a dog—

so parched, the tongue is hanging out the side of its mouth, literally panting for water. Unattractive, huh?

Well, this is the image I believe many people that are so obviously uncomfortable in their Singleness give off. It dictates everything you do and say, what you wear, the places you go—every aspect of your life is centered on finding 'love'. This desperation can be focused on one certain person or just a relationship in general. In fact, many people are actually in love with the idea of being in love. They are usually willing to lower their standards, or not set any, for the sake of belonging to someone. Like a gold ring in a pig's snout, so is a woman with no discretion[84]. In this case, you are a woman—so beautiful, unique and wonderfully made, yet no realization of the value that you possess. Vow no longer to cast your pearls to swine[85]. God worked hard to develop everything that he took you through into a priceless pearl. For you to present it to someone who doesn't respect your value, who wouldn't know how to appreciate it, is a direct insult to God. Until you know your worth, no one else will.

Jesus is the only man worthy of being chased. And He is the only man that the more you chase Him, the more He allows you to catch Him, and He pursues you right back. My pastor coined the term "pursuit is the evidence of desire". Anything a man wants, he will be willing and ready to pursue. If you had to pursue him, you may always experience doubt and insecurity because he didn't choose

---

[84] Proverbs 11:22

[85] Matthew 7:6

you—he simply accepted your choice. Big difference. If he pursued you, then he recognized something he wanted and went after it. If he conceded to your pursuits, he may be still looking for the one that is worth him pursuing.

With that being said, ladies we have to understand that just because a man finds us, doesn't mean we have to choose him. You still have a choice. If the man who has 'found' you is not worthy of your favor, you have the right and responsibility to not settle and to hide yourself again in Christ until one worthy comes in pursuit. Half a man is not better than no man, and until you've had a real one, you might be tempted to believe this bull. Remember, you know your worth; don't forget it for the sake of belonging with just anyone.

You have the power to move on; activate it. Remember the example of Saul and David. Your king needs you to move on so you can be free to accept his love. Learn how to recognize when a man doesn't really want you and refuse to just be a placeholder. If he didn't want you at first and when your interest in him starts to wane, then all of a sudden he starts showing you all of this attention—be careful. More likely than not, he didn't suddenly have an epiphany. He might just want to see if he can still get you. When you respond so readily (because although you verbally stated you were over him, you didn't do any of the hard work to actually get there), this lets him know the door is still open. Then when he decides not to walk through it, this will leave you thinking, "How could I have been so stupid"-again.

If he isn't calling, in most cases-he isn't just busy, he's not interested. Now, this does not apply to the situations in which only 24 hours have gone by or he is traveling on a mission trip in the Safari desert and you haven't heard from him. I am referencing the man that works an 8-5 and has a pretty normal day, yet you gave him your number (sometimes without being prompted), and he hasn't called in a week or two or three.

If a man is truly interested in you, you will be the highlight of his day, not a check off on his to-do list. Stop making excuses for a man that doesn't want you. Take your power back and move on to someone who does. It's OK to face rejection, its normal; and this will not be the last time you will experience it unless you are called to Glory. Learn from it and keep going. Christ needs you whole to fulfill His vision and your husband needs you complete to be his complement. Don't keep either of the true men in your life waiting longer than need be.

~A Word to the Brothers~

Being the head should be viewed as more of a righteous responsibility for your family than a glorified privilege to make self-centered decisions. This is a grave responsibility, because not leading your wife and family in the fashion she deserves will cause your prayers to be hindered[86]. Being male doesn't automatically mean you will know how to be the head. If you don't know because you didn't have a

---

[86] 1 Peter 3:7

father to teach you, set your pride aside and sit under a man who is where you want to be. Learn to be the head without being the dictator. Chromosomes make you a male, but character makes you a man. God wants you to be worthy of both labels.

The man should be the head, but many don't know what this looks or feels like, so they resort to leading with a strong arm instead of an open heart. This can be very detrimental to relationships. Be the spiritual leader, but don't be so 'spiritual' that you can't learn from her wisdom. Guys, it's best to make decisions after careful consideration of how it will affect your wife and family—before it's made. A man that can't admit that he is wrong, may not be much of a man. A woman who understands her role has no problem with submission if she knows you're being led by Christ. Reassure her by praying for her and with her. In so doing, this keeps the relationship balanced. Keep in mind, the head nourishes the body, so remember to lead her to the throne and wash her with the Word of God.

Are you looking to chase or are you prepared to pursue? To pursue implies an intentional, conscious, and wholehearted effort to obtain something. To chase is to follow rapidly with the intent of capturing. I liken this to the scenario of buying a new car. When you decide you are in the market for a new car, but aren't sure what you want, you may go to several dealerships and test drive anything from a Ford to a Cadillac. You know you want something, but you don't have all of the specifics in mind, so you keep looking until you find the one you believe has the best features for you. This is typical, but not often the case when you are in the market for a luxury car. When you have decided your next car will be the Infiniti QX56 Black on Black with moon roof, chrome wheels, and midnight black chrome grille you don't need to test drive anything else. You will drive right past the Ford, Cadillac, and even the BMW dealership because you know exactly what you want. You have done your homework and you know what it will take to get this vehicle. When you get to the dealership, the only reason you will need to test drive it is to introduce yourself because you already know her. Are you following me? Every woman deserves to be that Infiniti—not the random vehicle you buy at the spur of the moment. Pursuing her treats her like the jewel she is, chasing her does not.

Since pursuit is the evidence of desire, this means you are prepared to wait for her favor. Boys chase a casual girlfriend or a 'special friend', men pursue a wife. Are you prepared to pursue or are you just desperate for a chase? You can always tell a man who is not accustomed to dealing with a woman who knows her worth. He will do one of two things: step his game up to be worthy of her favor or back down and look for an easier prey. It's best to figure out which category you fall in, before a woman has to tell you.

What may be hard to understand is that we don't need you to fix everything. For many things, we just need you to be there, that's it. Your arms hold a special power that we don't even know how to put into words. Hold her as she cries, even if you don't understand why. Listen when she complains about her day or tells you about a puppy she saw in the road. Laugh when she tells a joke that isn't funny. We know you would probably prefer we ask our girlfriends how we look in an outfit, but we crave hearing your affirmation.

The same way we feel rejected, we understand that you face it as well. The way we deal with it however, is often different. A woman may try to convince you that you need to be with her, but many times the man will cover the rejection by downplaying the initial interest. Stop getting upset if a woman is not interested in you. Be happy that she didn't take your number and throw it in the nearest trash can when she walked away, or blocked your number after you made her store it in her phone, and then call you so you would have hers.

Just in case you hadn't noticed, every Black woman is not angry, bitter, selfish, demanding, stuck up, loud, ghetto, a gold digger, or the typical "baby mama." Some of us may just see what you have to offer and it's not what we will accept in a man. Use it as a learning tool and do what it takes to be worthy of the next one you approach.

Contrary to some beliefs, we are not always the problem. I was told by a guy friend of mine that a man doesn't pass up a pot of gold. Instead of telling him how stupid he sounded, I simply said, "The problem may not be with us (being that I am Single, I fall into that category), but the men that claimed to 'find us' weren't worth being found by, so we intentionally threw ourselves back into the sea."

Another imperative tidbit of information is that if you are really determined to pursue, once you get her, keep doing the things that were needed to catch her. Men and women alike can become too comfortable in relationships; continue to make her feel special. I know the focus usually goes to a woman letting herself go after getting in a relationship, but truth be told you may need to get up and go to the gym with her. If you opened every door that she walked through while you pursued her, don't change this once she is yours. It doesn't take a lot to win most women hearts, but once you have lost it, it is nearly impossible to get it back without divine intervention.

As a man, this may be hard to hear and even harder to accept, but it has to be said. God may have allowed your wife to be abused by another man so you could restore her faith in all men. This will not be an easy task, and you should be well aware that there will be times you will want to walk away. You may have to love her past the scars another man caused. She will need restoration from a good man before she can let go of the hurts of a bad one. Some men come to restore and this may be your calling in her life. Don't give up on her if you truly love her. Honor her, respect her, cherish her, and don't let her go. Fight fair. Don't be quick to leave; fight for her not just with her.

A good woman isn't hard to find, it just takes a good man to stop chasing the superficial and really pursue her.

Likewise, a good man isn't hard to find, it just takes a good woman to slow down, sit down, and stop looking for him.

~From the Inside Out~

If we put too much value on the outside, we will miss the inside every time. I'm not saying lower your standards in the physical appearance department, I'm just advising to be a bit more realistic. I have been the superficial person that dated a fine dude that I couldn't have a fairly intelligent conversation with. I literally would think about a certain subject before I started speaking, choosing my words carefully because I wasn't sure if he would understand some that I use in everyday language. Now, I'm not saying that he was unintelligent; just that we weren't on the same level in that field and I couldn't discuss things as freely as I would have liked with him. That experience taught me to be more realistic and not just focused on a cute face and thick waist (yep, females appreciate thickness as well). What am I trying to get you to realize? Simple. I don't know anyone that throws away the present just to keep the wrapper. If you are too afraid to open the present because you don't know what you will find, your standards may be a bit warped. Everything that glitters…well you know the rest.

The things needed to sustain a relationship aren't always those that are seen on the surface. I'm not telling you to go look for the down and out brother or to try to get with only the homely girls. But, I am saying that if our grip is too tight on what we think we want, we aren't leaving room for God to give us what we really need. I can almost guarantee your blessing will not come in the package that you have on your list, but I can guarantee that it will exceed your expectations.

Remember, the only place where baggage flies free are on airlines (and not even many of those). Let go of your past relationships so you can get to what God has in front of you. If you are not over your ex, don't drag someone else along for the ride. Close that door before you open the next. It's impossible to compete with a ghost, and unfair to ask your future spouse to do it. Allow your potential mate to make their own mistakes—not pay for someone else's.

I once heard a joke and didn't see how it had any underlying meaning until I started to write this book. A woman goes to the doctor and tells him her body is broken because everywhere she touches hurts. She touches her head, "Ouch," her leg, "ouch," and her stomach, "ouch—see, I told you!" she exclaims to the doctor. The doctor examines her and says, "Your body isn't what's broken, your finger is." Moral of the story: if you are trying to figure out why every relationship you have been in didn't work out, maybe your answer lies in examining yourself. You were the only constant in each of them. Fix your issues so that you can be whole, lacking nothing[87].

I end with the beginning: how do you know if you are ready? Evaluate yourself by asking, "When I have

[87] James 1:4

determined that I want something so bad, how will I respond if I don't get it? What do I do if it doesn't come in the way or the timing I think it should? How am I responding in my waiting season?" These answers will speak to your spiritual maturity in accepting God's will for your life and may give you answers regarding your readiness to move into the next season. If you have been crying out to Jesus for direction in this area and still haven't heard an answer, maybe God is saying, "Hold on because I'm still preparing you both—you'll know when you're ready."

The Covenant: Ruth and Relationships

But Ruth replied, "Don't urge me to leave you or turn back from you. Where you go I will go, and where you stay I will stay. Your people will be my people and your God my God,"
~Ruth 1:16 NIV

We all have a childhood dream that when there is love, everything goes like silk, but the reality is that marriage requires a lot of compromise.
~Raquel Welch

For the conclusion of this book, we will discuss a common story in the Bible that models what we have often been told is the correct example of a relationship, the book of Ruth. Many remember the fairytale ending and fail to focus on what happened before that. Esther is a similar story; people remember when she saved her people, but they often forget the obedience, struggles, and sacrifice which came before it.

The story of Ruth is often only told in light of her being found by Boaz, but there is so much more that God wants to reveal in this book. I believe if we break it down into sections, we can get the essence of Christian dating/courtship (which ever word you would like to use), leading up to a God ordained marriage. We will end with this analysis, but we will begin by talking about unrealistic expectations in marriage.

~You Want a Wedding but You Will Get a Marriage~

Getting married with unrealistic expectations will lead to real disappointments. Marriage, or any relationship for that matter, can't be based merely on the butterflies in your stomach. Remember love is a decision. If you get married before you have fully understood the magnitude of this decision, the first day that you wake up and don't feel those butterflies—you will want to flee. You will be more susceptible to temptation and you have just given the enemy a foothold. The butterflies may highlight your wedding, but the decision will determine your marriage.

After the wedding is when reality sinks in and you realize this is the person that you are meant to be with for the rest of your natural life. This can be a very sobering thought if you have never really weighed the seriousness of your decision. This is evidenced when either spouse says, "You are not the person that I married." That's not entirely true. You married the representative and didn't bother to really get to know the person. That is who you married, you just dated the representative.

Many women plan more for the wedding than the marriage, walking into it totally unprepared. After the honeymoon and the two weeks of what may seem like constant gratification of guilty pleasures (without the guilt, might I add), you are no longer a bride—you are a wife.

(Scary music playing in the background): are you ready for that? Do you even understand what a wife is? It's OK as a Single to admit that you don't, but you would want to figure it out before you get to the altar. Although there may be a slight learning curve as you both get accustomed to cohabitation, there is no training period where someone will come into your home with a manual and slideshow of the duties of a wife. Your mother, his mother, and even a marriage mentor may be there to help and assist you, but when your front door is closed, it's ultimately up to you and God to wing it.

Titus 2:4-5 states that the "older women should urge the younger women to love their husbands and children, to be self-controlled and pure, to be busy at home, to be kind and to be subject to their husbands, so that no one will malign the Word of God." A wife is supposed to be lowly (not your position, but your attitude), submissive, and serving to her husband. The wedding day may seem to be all about you, but the marriage is a shared spotlight (and at times, you may be playing the background). Realistically understand this and be prepared.

Are you realistic even in your ideals of a marriage for that matter? Have you asked the hard questions? What if he cheats? What if you cheat? No one goes into a marriage saying they will cheat, but yet it happens—alot. How would you handle it? Is the marriage immediately over, or do circumstances and motives play a part in the decision? Have you discussed when you want to have kids? These are all very real concerns and many that most dating couples don't broach for fear of popping the "butterflies and sweet nothings" bubble. If you don't choose to deflate it and somberly consider the life choice you think you are so ready to make, that bubble will pop on its own, and it will take every ounce of your faith, God's grace, along with the prayers of others to keep you from popping with it.

Marriage may be easy to enter, but it should be harder to leave, by Biblical standards. The Bible warns about entering into marriage lightly and to not be unequally yoked, but ultimately it is your decision when you get married and who you get married to. But once you are married, remember the stipulations for what God calls "justified divorce." God doesn't recognize "irreconcilable differences" as grounds for divorce. Many of those differences were there before you got married; you just refused to acknowledge them.

I would like to speak of a familiar scripture that we often quote, but I don't know if we have really analyzed the true meaning behind it. Proverbs 18:22 states, "He who finds a wife finds a good thing and inherits the favor of the Lord." Now most Christians know this scripture, but have you ever researched it for yourself? We have been taught that this clarifies that the man is supposed to find the wife, and we use it to justify why a woman should not be looking for a man. On the surface level, this is one interpretation of the scripture, but it goes so much deeper than just this.

Let's break it down:

He: On first thought, this is to mean just a man, but looking deeper, this is the same he that is used to describe Adam, Joseph, and David. This he (he is "whoso" in Hebrew and used in John 3:16) is not just a male, but also one who has the mental capabilities of agape love; one who is set financially, emotionally, mentally, and physically to provide for a wife. These traits are required to accept and receive love as God intended. This is the he who is prepared for the responsibility of a wife and a family. This is the man who separates himself and seeks wisdom from God. He is ready for the serious and great task of loving a woman as Christ loves the Church, respecting her and honoring her as the weaker partner. The mental capacity to love comes from many sources, but it is not based solely on emotions. (If love is only directed by emotions, then what happens when the butterflies fade away? What happens when, in the heat of an argument or the throes of lust with another person, you 'forget' that you made a conscious decision to love your spouse? If it were merely an emotion, the divorce rate would be a lot higher.) This he is one who is serving the Lord in full capacity now, as a Single male. From this interpretation, many males don't fit the characteristics of the he, so therefore may not be ready to start looking.

That Finds: Now, this word is interesting because the original Hebrew does not take from the definition of the act of physically searching for something. Even Webster has the right definition: to discover or perceive after consideration; to come upon by chance; to become aware of, or discover (oneself), as being in a condition or location. WOW! This means if you are in your lane seeking the Lord, then you may happen to come upon or discover your wife or husband to be (while in your lane, going in the same direction). Joseph was given his wife. Likewise, Adam and David did nothing to deserve their wives but were given them. You should be directly focused on pursuing God, traveling the path He has set. When you are in the right location and condition, God will awaken you from your slumber, and you may happen upon that appointed person.

A Wife: Now, this is not referring to just a female, but a woman who is worthy of such an honorable name. A wife is esteemed, so therefore this label will not apply to all women. This wife is a jewel of great value, a rare jewel. He has found that one who will not only contribute more than anything to his comfort and satisfaction in this life, but will push him in the way to heaven. This means if you are not praying and serving God now while a Single woman, you probably won't magically start when you get married. It also refers to taking care of the responsibilities of the household and fulfilling your wifely role: cooking, cleaning, caring for the family, etc. (For those of you who are all for the Women's Movement, Woman Liberations, Women's Equal Responsibilities and Roles, it may work [and should] in Corporate America, but has no relevance or authority over God's Word pertaining to the home and marriage. We still have roles, as evidenced in the scriptures of Proverbs 31:10-31, Titus 2:4-5, Ephesians 5:22, and 1 Peter 3:1-6. I didn't write it, I'm just quoting it.) This definition also has to do with the man's capacity to love that particular woman. "A good wife" is a woman the man recognizes as one he can love. This is the woman he would protect and honor spiritually, mentally, emotionally, and physically at all costs, above everything, keeping God first.

Finds a Good Thing: Now, just because you are a female and you get married, doesn't mean that you will be a "good thing." In order to meet these qualifications, you have to first meet the criteria of a wife. That means you also have to have your stuff together; not just sitting around waiting on your life to start when "Boaz" shows up. To be found, you have to be traveling in the same direction that he is traveling; a path directed and ordained for God's glory. Proverbs 31:12 says, "She brings him good all the days of his life." So are you living as a good thing right now? The Hebrew goes on to infer that the only way a man can, from the innermost part of his soul, give his love to a woman is if he recognizes in her the ability to respond and accept his love. That's how women are designed by God—to be the responders of a man's love.

And Inherits the Favor of the Lord: This is one of those "if/then" clauses. If all the criteria are met, then you will receive the blessings afterward. Favor: granted to her and bestowed upon him; not by his own diligence, but by God's good providence. Meaning, you can't sway God's hand or speed up His timing, but when and if He so sees fit, He will bestow it upon you[88]. This is the beauty of God's Word. Just a small verse can be packed with so much of what He wants us to understand. I pray this will encourage you to add to your understanding of this scripture, as well as give you a reference to determine whether you are ready for this commitment.

~Seven Characteristics of a Godly Mate and Relationship~

The story of Ruth is often only told in light of her being found by Boaz, but there is so much more we need to know. Let's continue dissecting God's Word to better understand what we should be looking for, and also how we should carry ourselves. Take a look at these characteristics and see how you may be able to apply them within your life.

Commitment: When Ruth is introduced in this book, the first thing noticed about her is her commitment to both God and to Naomi. She forsook her desires for the Lord's direction. She gave up her family and entire life as she knew it, to follow God. This is the epitome of commitment.

[88] Adapted from Pastor Monty Rainey-Foundations for Marriage

Naomi had nothing to offer her but a life serving the God that Ruth had been introduced to thru her, and that was enough. Christ doesn't owe us anything; we are saved from hell because of His commitment to love us, not saved to receive the provisions of His hand. He calls for our commitment not because he can provide for us, but simply because He is the Way, and all of our provisions come from staying in His shadow. His favor and His blessings are added promises from Him along the way.

Character: Ruth's character preceded her. Before Boaz even spoke a word to her, he inquired about her. Whoever he asked, they spoke highly about her, even though she was a foreigner in a strange land. Because of her commitment, her character was evident in everything that she did. She was gleaning in fields to take on the responsibility that she could have walked away from, like her sister-in-law. Ruth's motive was to care for her mother- in-law, not to be seen or recognized for what she was doing. What would people hear about you if they ask someone who has been watching?

Communication: Ruth was committed to appropriate communication. She was open, honest, accountable, and submissive to her mentor and confidant. Many times we don't seek accountability because we don't want to tell everyone all the hard issues we face. I challenge you to fight this perception because it is not biblical. We were created to hold each other accountable, to rebuke, to restore and revive within the Word of God. Ruth gave clear information to her mentor and didn't hide the details. When asked where she had gleaned, she didn't just say, "Oh, well down the street." Give good communication because you never know what someone can add to the information you have gathered. When dating (or deciding to date), ask around about your potential. You shouldn't base your sole decision on the information you gather, but how the person is perceived may reveal something about their character.

Counsel: The Bible states that a man is wise who seeks wise counsel[89]. Ruth trusted Naomi's countenance enough to listen and heed her advice. She recognized her mentor had more experience than she possessed and wanted to learn from her. Don't seek wise counsel if you aren't going to use it. Find someone who is in the position you want to be in (strong in character, commitment, communication, and Christ), then commit to sit at their feet and glean from them.

Courage: Ruth took a huge risk by going to present herself at the threshing floor. If someone else would have seen her, or mistook her intentions, this could have hurt her witness and brought doubt to her virtue. When we submit to God, we have to risk everything we know to gain all that He will give us. Because she trusted her counsel, she had the courage to know it was sound advice and then act on it. Be cautious of your counsel and know that if God is your

---

[89] Proverbs 1:5; 12:15

Chief Advisor, He will not direct you outside the safety of His plan.

Courtship: Boaz made his intentions clear from the beginning. Ruth didn't have to guess his feelings or what the next steps would be. He was very clear on the direction of the relationship, and he acted as the head. He protected her virtue. A man ready for courtship will protect your virtue and favor above his own desires. He covers her. He will "fight" for what is his and will contend with anyone or anything that stands between them. Remember love always hopes and protects. If your potential mate is encouraging you to do ungodly stuff, that might not be love, but lust.

Ruth was restored by her kinsman and was eternally blessed by this covenant. Her divine appointment as Boaz's wife lined her up to be in the linage of Christ. The covenant was eternal, unbreakable. Others blessed the covenant because it was clear God orchestrated it. He used a Moabite and Rahab's (a prostitute) descendent to show how He will redeem us from any situation we are in.

If you remember nothing else from this chapter, understand that Christian marriage is a covenant relationship, not a contractual agreement. Covenants are not meant to be broken or to be entered into lightly. If we study Ruth in this light, God will show us how He is our Kinsman Redeemer and what we should wait for as women of God. He will also show what should be striven for as men of God to fully embrace godliness and all future blessings.

It has been my humblest pleasure to share my journey with you and encourage you to continue (or begin) enjoying this Single season of your life. Remember that God hasn't forgotten you. Commit to really get into your Singleness, before you get out of it. It's an honor and a privilege to be in the presence of the King; bask in knowing that He enjoys your company and He is pleased with you.

I believe that God does everything for His glory. So He will join your life with your husband or wife when He has gotten the maximum amount of glory out of your Single life. Take this to mean your Single life is bringing more glory to God's name than your married life would be at this moment. What an honor! Treat it as such.

If you are still Single and living for God, it just means that the Lover of your soul wants more time alone with you.

~Gratitudes~

So, I wrote a book. Who would have thunk it? Apparently the amazing God that I serve saw this moment before I was even formed, and for that I will be eternally grateful.

Thank you God, for Jesus.

Jesus Christ, I cannot thank you enough, not for what you have done, but for Who You are to me. You are my Savior, my Redeemer, my Lover, my Best Friend and my Confidante. My Liberator, you are my true Soul Mate, because my soul is forever tied to you. You are my 1st Husband and your place is firmly planted there. The Cross was for me, my life is for you. Where you go, I go and where you lead, I will chase after you—I have no other choice. As long as You give me a platform, I will use it to shout your praises and lift You high, drawing others to You.

To my family, both biological and by logic- I love you all dearly. There are too many of you to name individually, but know that you hold a special place in my heart. Thank you for your love, prayers, dedication and belief in me. Without you, much of this wouldn't have been possible. Mama, thanks for always being so proud of me, and being so ready to share that pride with any and every one that will listen. It means more than you know—I love you. Dear, I love you so much even if I don't always tell you, thanks for being the backbone of our family. Drink your water, love.

Thanks to all my mentors, mentees, friends, family, sorority sisters and fraternity brothers, church members and ministry co-laborers—you are forever in my prayers.

And to all of you reading this book- I thank you. Thank you for giving a young, inexperienced, new author a chance to speak to you on a timeless issue. My life has truly been a living testimony of Romans 8:28- all things work together for the good of those that love the Lord and are called according to His purpose. I'm a witness that they may not all be good-but if you hold on and faint not, you will eventually get to the sweet. Thank you, Lord, for bringing it full circle. I can't wait for what's next.

Keep reading for a sneak peak of NOT Another Devotional Book: Through My Eyes... Book 2 in the NOT Another Series...

~Last Remarks~

Thank you so much for sharing in my journey. I pray that this book has been as much of a blessing to you reading it, as it has been to me by writing it. I am still in this journey, or should I say that I am back in this journey with you, and God is showing me wondrous things along the way. I pray that you are motivated to get everything that God has for you in this season, before you leave it.

If you've gotten this far and this book has impacted you in any way, I'd be honored to hear it. Please consider leaving a review on Amazon of the book with your thoughts and biggest takeaways. As an independent author, reviews are our lifelines and connections to be found by others that could need this message as much as you did. *I read EVERY review and I'd love to celebrate with you.*

If after reading this book, you are still struggling with being satisfied during your Single season and would like me to stand in agreement with you, please contact me at one of the following:

It's a journey, and you don't have to travel it alone.

Connect with Me Online:
Twitter: www.twitter.com/mysingleseason
Facebook: www.facebook.com/authorlavoniartryon
Website:www.lavoniartryon.com
Email: lavonia@lavoniartryon.com

About the Author

LaVonia R. Tryon is an Author, Entrepreneur, Public Speaker, and Motivator. A dynamic speaker and session leader, La Vonia is known to captivate her audience with creative and vivid examples as well as humorous crowd interactions. Her unique insight into scripture and wholehearted desire to deliver the voice of God to Singles is evident in her daily lifestyle and her writing style.

A people helper at heart and by profession, LaVonia graduated with a Bachelor's of Arts in Counseling Psychology from Baylor University and a Master's within the same field from Alabama A&M University. She is the Founder of Healing Hands of HOPE (Holistic Opportunities for Personal Enrichment) a disability advocacy agency that trains educators and employees to work with individuals with disabilities.

When not writing and pursuing professional passions, LaVonia enjoys spending daily time with her 93yo grandma and her 4yo niece… they are both fireballs. She makes a mission to start every day on purpose and live it intentionally.

LaVonia's heart reaches for the Single that feels like they are missing out on something, or possibly missing something within themselves because they are still Single. Her goal and mission is touch every Single with the hope and joy locked in this season waiting for them to explore. She would love to share her heart with other ministries, churches, and groups as God allows her. If you would like for her to speak at your church, ministry or event-please send an email to lavonia@lavoniartryon.com.

NOT Another Singles Devotional

Sneak Peak

The 30-Day Journey to Revolutionize & Renew Satisfaction
in Your Single Season

SINGLE? At times this can seem like a four-letter curse word. When you get this dreaded question from family, friends, the random guy at Starbucks, it makes your insides cringe. What's worse is what usually follows your hesitant response. "Oh...you're SINGLE? Oh, ok. Well, just keep waiting, your someone will come." Sound familiar?

So that's what we do. We wait. And we wait. Then, we wait some more. Until hopefully, one day, we wake up and decide to ask the determining question: 'WHAT am I waiting for?' In that question, and the ensuing response, lies our freedom to enjoy this time. When we begin to look at our lives and decide that "waiting" requires action, we will start to look for the things that we should be doing in our Singleness.

What if this isn't your scenario? What if you are enjoying your Singleness, but it seems like it is lasting forever? Why is this Singles journey sometimes prolonged as if it is stop and go traffic? Just when we think a lane is opening up and we are making progress...we come to an abrupt stop and inch back to a standstill. I think this happens for a couple of reasons. One reason could be that our first single spell (or if you are like me-spells), only matured us to a fraction of our potential. We see, act and discern better than we did before, yet everything is not as clear as it could be.

Next, they (no one ever knows who "they" is) say that repetition is a key component of memorization or internalization. And that's what we want to do: internalize the Word and allow God to make us whole. I don't know about you, but once I realized that this time could and should be used as an opportunity to fall more in love with Christ, I was so fired up and ready to experience the fullness of this season with God, and the utmost desire to wholeheartedly serve the Lord while I waited. Little did I know that this period would be challenged.

When I first started to write this book, I had recently started a personal 30-day challenge; a detox from relationships, if you will and a feast on God. Then I met a guy, (where have you heard that before?), but I didn't think anything of it. During the challenge, I was so excited and in communion with the Lord that nothing progressed with said guy, because I was heavenly focused. Shortly after the challenge concluded, he made his move. He began to seduce me. (Note here: the Lord woos, the devil seduces-there is a big difference.) I'm not saying this guy was the devil - far from it. But he was used as a distraction, or maybe even a test, to see if I was truly ready to live the life I had just spent a month challenging myself, and inadvertently others, since it was carried out and followed on social media, to live.

But back to the fairy tale. This guy was great. At the beginning, who isn't, right? But, in retrospect he wasn't that great at all. He had flaws and a lot of them, but I refused to acknowledge them. Due to circumstances and me reading too much into just normal occurrences, I had deemed him "the one", with no input from God. I saw signs early on that he didn't treat me the way "the one" would, but I excused them and wrote them off as 'he's not there yet, but he's trying.' I hadn't internalized the fact that a man needs to be fully submitted to God before I could potentially submit to him. I was trying to make a husband out of him, when he hadn't allowed God to make a man out of him. Although it took me a while to fully let that go, I did.

In my first book, NOT Another Singles Book ©2011, I use the tagline 'my struggle – your lesson', to denote a time that I had to learn a lesson the hard way, all while you get to benefit from my experience without actually experiencing the pain. This was yet another example of 'my struggle-your lesson'.

In Mark 8:22-24, a blind man was presented to Jesus to be healed. Jesus spit on the man's eyes and asked him if he saw anything. His response is the premise for this entire book. "I see people, but they look like trees walking around," he said. First of all, he had to have known what trees were, to use this as a reference. I equate this to him being taught what trees were by a friend or teacher, being able to touch them and then imagine what they looked like, in his mind's eye. We can use the same example of what we believe to be the 'perfect relationship'. We are taught what they should look like through books, sermons, Singles conferences, speaking with other married couples; but we have never really experienced one, so we have a formed image in our mind's eye that may not be entirely accurate.

But that's not the point. The point is that he can see. Hallelujah, right? Wrong. He was healed but he wasn't whole. He was better than his previous condition, and he

209

should have been grateful for that. Why ask for more? Or should he? He is standing in the presence of The Answer, and he realized in that moment, that this was his moment to get whole, not just better. At his confession, Jesus 'once more' put His hands on the man's eyes and then his sight was restored and he saw everything clearly.

I challenge you to use this scripture as a baseline for this book. This is what we are waiting for. A 'once more'. A do over. A chance to detox from the superficial, shallow relationships of the world and feast on the supernatural, sanctifying relationship with our Savior. You are now in the presence of The Answer. Don't you dare live another day better, when you can be living to the fullest .

When Jesus healed the blind man, he spit on his eyes, touched them and then touched them again. Could Jesus have healed him in one touch. Of course, but I think he was staring into your future and realizing that you would need the encouragement that He imbedded in this story. You would need to see, that it's ok, not to be ok. That you don't have to settle for just being better, but you will be responsible for participating in your full healing. Your healing may be a process as well. If you allow it, and be honest with Christ, about where you are…there is no limit to what you will be able to now 'see'.

My only requirement for this book, is that you pray and open your heart to what God has to say to you. Even if you don't think that a particular day applies to you; meditate on it. I believe that God is going to share something fresh with you each day, just as He has for me.

All 30 days will include a brief devotional, a key scripture to memorize, a Psalm to read, and a challenge or task to do and evaluate about your Single season. Some may be new to you, and some may just be confirmation of a Word that the Lord has already given you.

Let's journey together…

DAY 1: The Single "Curse"-- Or So They Say

MEMORIZE: Psalm 37:23 The Lord directs the steps of the godly. He delights in every detail of their lives. NLT

READ: Psalm 37

CHALLENGE #1: Take time today to think about what you perceive to be the hardest thing to understand or accept about your Single season. Why is it hard for you to believe that you are already complete? Take a quiet moment to evaluate this and answer honestly. This will be your baseline.

The Bible-(AMP) says: 'The steps of a good man are directed and established by the Lord when He delights in his way (and He busies Himself with his every step) . This scripture is so rich because it reminds us that the Author and Perfector of our Faith is orchestrating our lives. Our steps are ordered, directed and established by the Lord Himself, meaning that we can't have a misstep, mistake or an oops without Him already knowing about it, and always having a plan in place to work it out for our good in the end. When He (big H denotes perfect Lord) delights in his (little h denotes imperfect man) way, He will busy Himself with his EVERY step. This Word brings tears to my eyes when I realize that the Creator of the universe will busy Himself around my life. That is mind-blowing to imagine that He cares that much about me. So, the very least that I can do is offer up my life as a sacrifice to Him.

If every step is ordained because we are living a life that is striving to please Him daily, then He Himself must have ordained our Singleness. That puts a different spin on it. Whether you are single with no prospects, single and dating, exclusively in a relationship but not yet engaged or even engaged to be married- you are still single, and you are right where God is ordaining you to be. You are in His will at this moment, which is the safest and sweetest place to be.

But, let's be honest, sometimes it doesn't feel sweet. Sometimes it is downright awful...and lonely...and tiring...and sad. Trust me, I know. I've been there, and I still have those days, but they have become fewer and fewer because I have now realized that I am in His will. Now I rest in the fact that even when it's not good, it's working for my good. And that makes it worth it. Just remember 'if it ain't good, then He ain't finished'.

There is beauty in desiring to stay in God's will, even when we don't understand it or desire the path that we are on. We desire His will for our lives more than we desire our comfort or the plan that we believe we should be living. Rest in that. You are exactly where you are supposed to be. God hasn't forgotten you, nor can He misplace you, because He is busy with ordering your every step. You are not His keys, or His eyeglasses--you are the beautiful jewel in His crown, the Heir to His righteousness, worthy of trading His Son's perfect life for your imperfect one. He's got you. Chill out. Are you ready to experience the fullness of this unique Season in your life?

DAY 2: Contentment isn't a Destination...it's a Journey

MEMORIZE: Exodus 13:17 When Pharaoh let the people go, God did not lead them on the road through the Philistine country, though that was shorter. For God said, "If they face war, they might change their minds and return to Egypt." NIV

READ: Psalm: 73 Focus on 1-3, 21-28

CHALLENGE #2: Take the long way today. Go a different, longer route home, to work, to church, school - walk a different path to class. Park at the furthest parking spot from the building and walk. Spend this extra time asking God to give you His eyes to see what He would show you. What does God reveal to you today?

This challenge is one of my favorites, and one that God continually shows me that I need to apply consistently. I had it in my head, but my heart at times still struggles with grasping the concept of trusting Him completely. When I first wrote this challenge, I made a conscious decision to walk to work instead of drive, (I was working really close to my house at this time) and as I walked, I asked God to give me His eyes. He showed me birds resting on a building. They had no worries, because they had no needs. At that moment, God reminded me that if I would just trust

Him, my worries would go away as well. He assured me that He has already supplied my needs and my only responsibility is to trust Him. I think we can all agree that this is much easier said than done. I had to realize that I am just as much in this journey as I am leading those that are following me. My struggles with contentment have become my platform to show others how to combat the loneliness, doubt, and feelings of worthlessness, and those dreaded "bad days" -- because I was experiencing them as well.

Many Single people struggle with contentment. What does it really mean to be content in Christ? How can you be content with Christ while you still wholeheartedly long for a mate? Am I telling God that He's not enough for me because I desire marriage so strongly? These (or some variations) are the questions that many Singles go to bed with at night, and still wake up with in the morning, to no answer. I've learned that what we perceive as silence, is often the answer to our prayers...

"Trust Me."

These two Words are whispered to our hearts so softly, and if we aren't careful, the shouting of our own desires will drown them out. God wants us to trust Him, WITH EVERYTHING, especially our desire to be married. When God is silent, it's not because He isn't there. God speaks even in the silence. When you can't see His face, can't feel His heart, or even discern His will -Trust HIS Purpose.

Jeremiah 29:11 (this will be a memory verse later in this challenge) says "I know the thoughts that I think towards you, thoughts of peace and not of evil, to give you a hope and an expected end." Even when He doesn't seem to speak, you are still on His mind and remember He is BUSY with your every step.

When the Israelites were released from Egypt, God lead them the long way, because He knew their hearts weren't strong enough to face war yet. In the same way for us Singles, delay is not denial. God recognizes that it takes longer to get Egypt out of us than to get us out of Egypt. You may be physically out of that last relationship, last sin, last misstep, but in your mind, you're still there. There are certain habits and issues you are still dealing with that God can't allow you to take into your Promised Land. Because He is a God of movement, He will take us on a detour to get to where we need to go, while He works that Egypt mentality out of us.

God knew that the Israelites would have run back into their slave situations if they saw even the prospect of war, because they still had the slave mindset. Likewise, you may not be ready for that. You may not be strong enough to stand and fight for your peace, for your contentment, for your joy – for whatever it is that the enemy will use to convince you that God has forgotten you; so, God desires to lead you around it. It will take longer, but there is so much beauty in the journey that you might never see if you just rush into a relationship.

I still had Egypt mindsets. The relationship that I recently ended before beginning to write this devotional more than confirmed that. I had gotten so comfortable in being Single that I became complacent in growing in this season. I got lazy and began to believe that I was "there"; that I had it all together. And this is where I fell. I was so convinced that I would be able to recognize "the one" when he came, so I couldn't bring myself to acknowledge that I had gotten it wrong - that he wasn't the one that I had been waiting for. I started to make excuses for him and even worse, to excuse him to treat me like less than I deserved. I still had an Egypt mindset, but my God has too much purpose planned in my future ministry to allow me to mess it up by settling for someone that was not MY promise. I was still dealing with balance, struggling not to replace the King of my eternal soul, with the king of my earthly life. So that ended, yet another lesson learned.

I had to recognize what my Egypt mindsets were if I ever wanted to get free. I gave too much too soon. I didn't speak up the first time that I felt disrespected, unconsidered, or an option instead of a priority. I let massive things slide to keep the illusion of peace. I compromised my standards because I was too afraid of admitting that I had read it wrong. These were my Egypt mindsets that God had to work out of me so that I wouldn't poison my Promised Land. This relationship was my detour around a sure war zone, and He knew if He would have brought "the one", then I would have allowed those old mindsets to cause undue stress and hardship. So, he allowed me to circle around the mountain for a little while longer until He knew that I would appreciate it, when I

218

crossed over. I understand this now, and I'm grateful that His plan is so much greater than my temporary pleasures.

What are your Egypt mentalities that God is using Singleness to prune out of you, so that you will be complete and made perfect, lacking nothing ? What old habits (sexual immorality, lust, anger, greed, idolatry, selfishness) are you still struggling with that God won't allow to pollute the Promised Land of marriage?

Delays are for our benefit, not for our harm. Use this journey to find contentment through preparation, tests and training. Allow God to prepare you for marriage, if that's in His will for you. And if it's not, then this preparation will enable you to be a better Single, souled out for His glory.

God honors and protects marriage-because it is the only direct symbolism of Christ and the Church. If you aren't making a very good church right now as a lady- and men, if you don't even resemble Christ - you are not ready. Stay in the journey, learn what you need, and then when it's God's time, walk into your Promised Land; whatsoever it may be.

DAY 3: God Loves Him Some You...So you should too!

MEMORIZE: Jeremiah 31:3 And the Lord appeared to us from afar saying, 'I have loved you with an everlasting love, I have drawn you to myself with loving kindness.'
NIV

READ: Psalm 139

CHALLENGE #3: Pamper yourself. Treat yourself to a nice lunch today. Give yourself a pedicure or spend some time just relaxing at the spa. Open yourself a cold root beer and enjoy the afternoon breeze on the patio. Take a long bath with candles and scented oils. Turn off the TV, sign out of Twitter, off Facebook, log off the 'Gram and just be with yourself. Spend some time today just being with you. Go on, you deserve it.

God loves Him some you. If He had a wallet, your picture would be in it. You would be highlighted on His refrigerator. He'd wear a shirt every day with your picture on the front and "PROUD PAPA" on the back. He loves you- completely, unconditionally, irrevocably loves you. At times, this is hard to grasp-that the Maker of the entire universe just wants to spend time with you. God wants to commune with you -- put your feet up, let your hair down and just talk.

This challenge really gave me some perspective. I missed Jesus. I had allowed the busyness of life to push away the presence of God. I was too involved in ministry, work, and 'my man', to steal away with God and get ministered into by my Savior. I was running on empty, ministering from yesterday's manna, and because I have so much Word stored up in me, no one noticed. If you have been saved a while and have grown to a certain level of maturity, you know that you can operate, serve and even minister out of a reservoir. You haven't spent quality time with God for days, weeks, sometimes even months, but you are still ministering off the overflow that you have stored up. Only the transparently honest will admit to doing it, and I was one. I knew that I could minister and pull an appropriate Word for someone, even when I hadn't been feed in a while. And although no one could tell, I suffered for it. I was spiritually weak and Kingdom ineffective because I was trying to use yesterday's manna for today's tasks. It didn't work for the Israelites, so there was no way that it would work for me. Oh, but when I got back into the presence of God-it was the sweetest thing. I never want to operate from that reservoir again. I long to spend fresh time with Christ daily -- whether 10 minutes or 2 hours-I need manna for each day.

But that's a perfect world. Often times, we don't "find time" to do it. We feel like prayer or quiet time is a chore that we need to fit into our life instead of a time that we get to cast the cares of our world, cares that we have been carrying on our shoulders, onto a broader Back. If Christ could carry the sins of the world and still get up with all power in His hands, surely He can handle whatever is keeping you stressed out.

Therefore, today's challenge is to just let it go. Spend some time relaxing -- not thinking, not worrying, not planning out your five-year strategic plan for success — just being with yourself. I've found that these are the times that I meet God walking in my garden, when I can get back to the cool of the day . His presence is always there, we just drown it out with our busyness.

Before I understood the difference between being alone and being lonely, I used to find it difficult to just be with me. I always had to be doing something: cleaning, cooking, washing clothes, reading, etc. Now, none of these things are bad things, and they all should be done, but when we use them to avoid spending some quality time with ourselves, it becomes a hindrance to our spiritual growth and getting to know ourselves in light of God's vision. As we saw yesterday, our perspective changes when we ask God to "give us eyes to see".

You should miss YOU. I know I did when I was on a journey of finding myself. We are never lost; I believe we are just hidden under all the lies, conformity, expectations, and fears that others place on us and that we often place on ourselves. I don't think we can truly know ourselves unless we spend some time alone with ourselves. In those quiet alone times, God downloads into you a vision, peace, guidance and direction, and you begin to realize that you don't have to work so hard for something that your Daddy already has and WANTS to give to you. You just have to be receptive and ready to receive it. God is waiting on you. What are you waiting on?

I missed me when I was in my relationship. I guess I still hadn't completely learned that balance, so I started sacrificing "me time" for "we time". And because the guy that I was with had a lot freer time than I did, that left no time for myself. That's another Egypt mindset that the Lord is ridding me of. You can't lose yourself in a relationship, otherwise you will be back on the journey of discovering yourself again when the relationship is over. And if the relationship leads to marriage, you will drain your spouse while you desperately try to search for yourself again. Take it from me...my struggle-your lesson.

Meet Him in the quiet place and share with someone what He deposits into you about yourself today.

NOT Another Singles Devotional is live on Amazon. Get your copy here.

Made in the USA
Monee, IL
28 June 2021